Does it feel like the honeymoon is over? Welc
jarring moment when reality hits and starry-ey
just how different they are! Thankfully, Kari ha
Marriage. With hope and humor, she coaches fl ᵧ ᵧ ᵤcouples to address
their disagreements, embrace their differences, and thrive as a team.

DR. GREG SMALLEY, vice president of marriage and family for Focus on the Family

If you are looking for a dry, heady book that will get lost on your shelf,
move on. But if you are looking for a book that is transparent and
vulnerable—rich with wisdom and full of heartfelt insight—then you
are holding the right book. Kari Trent Stageberg is the real deal. She has
embraced marriage, mothering, and life in the midst of all the ups and
downs, and she understands how to help married couples shrink big,
intimidating mountains through small moments of change.

DR. GARY AND BARB ROSBERG, marriage coaches and authors of *The 5 Love
Needs of Men and Women*

Something counselors learn that can powerfully change lives is helping
people put a name to the huge challenge they're facing. *The Merge for
Marriage* is not just a way to name and bring incredible insight to the
challenges of marriage—it's a whole book full of "we can do this!" tools
to guide couples toward greater commitment and greater closeness. Get
some couples around you who are facing the Merge and read and put into
practice the principles in this book.

JOHN TRENT, PHD, president of StrongFamilies and coauthor of *The Blessing*

If you're newly married or have been married for a few years, you'll want
to read *The Merge for Marriage*. This book shows you how to leverage
the inevitable challenges you face in merging your two lives so that your
differences actually bring you closer together. Kari has a fun, vulnerable,
and practical approach. You'll love this book.

DRS. LES AND LESLIE PARROTT, bestselling authors of *Saving Your Marriage
Before It Starts*

Kari provides insights, tools, and strategies to help couples get on the same page and work through their challenges. This book is a must-have if you are looking for a new way of overcoming the gridlock and patterns that keep you hurt and divided. If you are looking to bring real joy back into your relationship, you will find the answers in the timeless and life-giving truths that Kari presents.

ROLFE AND LEA CARAWAN, founders of Transformed Living

The Merge for Marriage is outstandingly practical and outrageously entertaining. It's easy to trust someone's advice when they share the most vulnerable and redeeming pieces of their journey. You'll see yourself in the book, see your spouse differently, and have hope for a beautiful Merge.

JILL MONACO, founder and CEO of Jill Monaco Ministries

Many in-love and engaged couples have short-term wedding dreams and long-term relationship goals. However, the process of getting from one to the other can test even the healthiest of relationships. In *The Merge for Marriage*, you will find insight to understand your spouse and your goals. Kari's wisdom and practical tools, such as your own customizable Merge Map, will leave you more prepared, encouraged, and inspired to meet your long-term relationship goals.

HALEY SCULLY, senior director of strategic and international operations for Hope for the Heart

With a solid plan and an understanding that we are able to leverage our strengths instead of living with friction, *The Merge for Marriage* provides a step-by-step plan for couples to come together and have a successful Merge. A must-read for all couples merging together!

GJ REYNOLDS, author and coach

You know that couple you look at and think, *I wish I had something like that*? Kari and Joey Stageberg are such people for me. The book you hold will get you *there*—to a place that makes others wonder how *you* have such a great marriage. Kari's fun style makes it easy to read a book that addresses complex challenges. And the ideas, exercises, and lessons make her principles easy to apply. Whether you are in your first few days of marriage or the first few decades, this book will launch you toward your dream of a marriage that fits you and your spouse.

    DR. MOLLIE BOND, author of *Hopelessly Hopeful*

Weddings are beautiful celebrations of love as two lives become one—so why do a shocking number of couples fail within months? Perhaps they don't know how to map the merge of ideas, personalities, and core values into oneness. *The Merge for Marriage* provides a technique and a literal map that can save countless marriages from experiencing pain. I recommend that every marriage add the powerful communication techniques found in *The Merge for Marriage* to move from conflict to connection.

    DWIGHT BAIN, founder of The LifeWorks Group

My wife and I have been married for forty years, yet I still discovered several useful tools in *The Merge for Marriage*. It would've been great to have this book thirty-five years ago, but better late than never! I encourage you to take hold of the jewels of information within this book and incorporate them into your current relationship, no matter how long you've been married.

    MATTHEW WARD, singer, songwriter, producer, and founder of Matthew Ward Ministries

Turning Frustration and Disunity
into Closeness and Commitment

THE MERGE

for

MARRIAGE

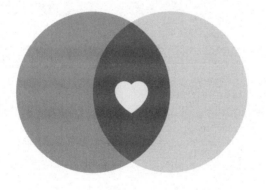

KARI TRENT STAGEBERG

FOCUS
ON THE FAMILY.

*A Focus on the Family resource
published by Tyndale House Publishers*

Contents

To Joey, the love of my life:

I would not be who I am, or where I am, without you, your uncondi-
tional love, and the way that you model health, strength, and Jesus in
our home. I hope and pray we get fifty more years to love, merge, and
enjoy life together.

To Lincoln:

You are our greatest blessing. May you always know that when it comes
to your dad and me, "forever our name, eyes, and heart" will be there.
I love you, my son.

Also, to my mom, dad, and sister:

You've all worked hard as encouragers and editors, and I could not have
done this without you. Thank you for your advice, wisdom, and sleep-
less nights right alongside me.

And last, but not least, to Denny and Judy:

Without your support, watching JT, and raising such a great man (who
is now my husband), none of this would exist. I can't thank you enough.

PART ONE

Meet the Merge

That First Life-Altering Merge Moment

When most people picture marriage, they think of a grand adventure with their best friend. Having a partner to do life with. Lots of laughter. Eventually a few kids will arrive, or a couple of dogs, or maybe both. And someday, if Dave Ramsey's financial wisdom liberates millennials from their avocado toast and crippling student-loan debt, they'll have a house of their own. Here they'll enjoy romantic dinners together, gazing lovingly into each other's eyes. Afterward, they'll sit snuggled together on the couch while watching their favorite show.

Yes, there will be some challenges here and there, but it won't be anything their love can't survive. Their love is going to last. *Forever.*

A lovely picture, to be sure. And it's all true. Really. For a few weeks, at least. Or, if you're fortunate, a few months.

But soon enough, *it* happens. The moment that changes everything.

The Merge.

When the Merge Hits Your Home

For me, that moment came quietly and unexpectedly during our third week of marriage.

It was a beautiful October day in the Pacific Northwest. The sun was out. Colorful leaves danced in sync with the wind. Happy couples drank pumpkin spice lattes while walking hand in hand along the waterfront. All was right with the world.

To make it even better, my husband, Joey, had just finished moving all his important stuff into the house that I had been renting prior to our wedding. We were now both officially home.

Thrilled that the moving process was finally over, I stopped by the grocery store to pick up some items for a celebratory dinner. I couldn't wait to get home and start cooking together and then jump into our nightly tradition of board games, laughter, and newlywed bliss.

However, nothing could have prepared me for the scene I was about to see upon arriving at our new home. Trying out my best Ricky Ricardo voice, I opened the door to our house and yelled, "Joey, I'm home!"

Almost immediately, a bright light popped around the corner, blinding my eyes. After a moment of stunned silence, I realized the light was attached to a head. My husband's head.

Joey's blond hair was sticking out haphazardly, and he waved at me with a big grin. His enthusiastic wave showcased big yellow rubber gloves that covered his arms all the way up to his elbows. The kind of gloves that reminded me of my grandma when she would pull out her cleaning kit on the last day of Thanksgiving weekend. With glove-covered hands and fierce determination in her eyes, my grandma would attack the bathroom, trying frantically to erase the damage that twelve people—sharing one toilet during the biggest food holiday of the year—had caused.

"What are you doing?" I asked with laughter.

"Cleaning!" he replied joyfully.

"Cleaning?" I repeated.

"Yep!" Joey replied.

"With a headlamp?" I pressed further. A confused look began to replace my smile.

"You know it!" he said confidently, as if cleaning with a headlamp were a completely normal activity that he did daily.

"Did the puppies get sick or something?" I asked, referring to our dogs and searching hard for a reason why either a headlamp or gloves would be needed.

"Nope, just cleaning the downstairs sink," he replied casually.

Cleaning the downstairs sink? That's when it hit me. I realized that I had absolutely no idea whom I had married. I know that may sound overly dramatic, but bear with me for a second.

Have you ever had a moment with your spouse when your differences seemed *so* pronounced that you questioned whether you even knew the person standing beside you at all? It's a moment when you start to think that maybe he or she has been lying to you the whole time about who they really are. You might even briefly wonder whether body-snatching aliens are in fact real and reason that they've decided to use your spouse as a host. Because nothing else could possibly explain your spouse's wacky, out-of-character behavior. Behavior that never made an appearance when you were dating.

This was that moment for me. *Who is this guy?* It certainly didn't help that, with the headlamp and the yellow granny gloves, Joey did kind of look like an alien.

What Does It Mean?

As Joey cheerfully went back to cleaning, I began to process the implications of the scene before me. My initial shock turned into worry as I began to wonder: First, was our sink really headlamp-level messy? After all, I had just cleaned it the week before. Second, did Joey normally clean with such precision and intensity? And, perhaps most importantly, would he expect *me* to clean with that much precision and intensity?

I would soon learn Joey's answers to the first two questions. Both were a resounding yes.

However, the answer to the third question remained to be determined. I had no idea what Joey would expect of me. Which meant that I had no idea how his cleaning standards would impact our relationship.

So a subtle but very real fear began to creep into my mind. What *were* Joey's expectations when it came to keeping our house clean? That fear produced more questions. What if I failed to live up to those expectations? What would all this mean for our marriage?

Fear of the unknown led to anxiety, and I began to imagine outrageous scenarios about living with Joey. Each scenario ended with me having to wear a hazmat suit around the house or sit on a couch covered in my great-grandmother's plastic couch cover. Or even—gasp—having to wash and put away my laundry *on the same day*!

As I thought about it further, I began to chastise myself for not seeing the warning signs earlier. A memory popped into my mind: One day, early in our relationship, Joey had surprised me by coming over and detailing my car. What I thought should have taken him an hour max took him—and I'm not exaggerating here—*six* hours.

At the time, it seemed like an amazing blessing. (And, I'll admit, ten months later, my car *was* still clean.) However, as I watched him clean our bathroom, I felt myself viewing his attention to detail and cleanliness differently.

Joey being a clean freak was no longer something that I could admire during the day and then avoid when he went home at night. The condition was permanent. The clean freak was living in my house, touching everything around me.

There was no place for me to escape.

Joey wasn't my boyfriend anymore. He was my husband. His cleaning habits didn't impact just him. They impacted me. And they would continue to impact me *foooorrrreeevvveerrrr* (said in my best Squints-from-*The Sandlot* voice).

Do You Remember That Moment in Your Relationship?

Maybe your first Merge Moment was something completely different. The first time you had to make a financial decision. Or when you realized you had different holiday traditions. Or when you watched your spouse handle conflict with in-laws.

Or maybe you're more like Joey and there wasn't one big moment but a series of smaller moments that highlighted your differences over time, your frustrations gradually building as those early weeks ticked by.

Whatever caused that discovery for you, we've all had a version of it. The moment (or series of smaller moments) when you recognize the full reality of the differences between you and your spouse—differences that you've committed to dealing with for the rest of your lives.

Noted marriage and family counselor Dr. John Gottman has probably studied more couples than anyone on the planet for his research on the reasons couples argue. His findings are illuminating. Gottman's team observed that there are generally two categories of disagreements between couples: solvable and unsolvable. A healthy relationship built around honesty and open communication can help couples resolve the first type of argument, but Gottman found that only 31 percent of arguments fit into this category. A whopping 69 percent of arguments that couples face are perpetual problems based on fundamental differences between them.[1] Wow! That means these differences aren't simply going to go away with good communication and healthy conflict resolution. Couples very often just look at things differently, and if they don't accept and even value those differences, they're in for huge challenges ahead.

Sometimes discovering these differences brings moments of joy, drawing us closer together. Our differences may even remind us *why* God brought our spouses into our lives in the first place.

Other times, these differences come across as potential threats. Especially when we realize that the differences may change the equilibrium in our relationship, or that they might require *us* to change.

It's possible to begin to see our differences in a way that can grow our relationship—making us, and our marriage, stronger. More on that later.

As for those differences in cleaning standards between Joey and me? Well, the issue certainly didn't go away overnight. As Dr. Gottman might observe, this one fell into the category of unsolvable disagreements. Joey and I began to notice many more of our differences in the weeks after the headlamp incident, especially when it came to cleaning. And we began to recognize how this one issue was fueled by other, larger differences in our personalities.

Here is how that looked for us.

The Joy of Cleaning

For me, having a clean house may be one of the greatest feelings in the world, but the actual *process* of getting the house clean is about as fun as a grade-impacting pop quiz on the first day of school.

I honestly dread cleaning. I wish I loved it, and it is on my prayer list of things that I'm asking God to change—along with helping me become a morning person and making green tea taste as good as coffee. *And please, God, allow popcorn to suddenly qualify as a fully nutritious meal.*

But for Joey, cleaning is truly a joyful experience—and often a musical one. As he works, he is belting out the lyrics to his personal playlist or singing boisterously to some soundtrack only he knows the words to.

The soundtrack of my cleaning experience consists mostly of me complaining, punctuated with an occasional grunt of frustration and, at times, some spiritually creative alternatives to cuss words. This soundtrack only grows in intensity when I notice how long the cleaning project is taking and how little progress I'm making.

Yes, this attitude is certainly on my prayer list as well.

The Precision of Cleaning

My primary goal with cleaning is to clean as fast as possible so I can get on to other, more important, things—things I actually want to be doing. However, whenever Joey asks me what those super important things are, I can't seem to find an answer good enough to help him see things my way. (If you've somehow cleared this hurdle with your clean-freak spouse, please stop reading and email me right now.)

Joey's goal with cleaning is to do it right. Not just *right*, but to a level of excellence that Mr. Monk would applaud—right before begging to move in.

Joey will walk by some household area that looks clean to me, shake his head, and then go grab the duster. And the vacuum. As Joey once explained, "You can't dust unless you vacuum. Because the dust spreads." Then, after a few minutes of intense and gleeful cleaning—after which the cleaned area looks exactly the same to me as it did before—he joyfully returns the duster and vacuum to their homes. (Homes that are clearly labeled, organized, and dust free.)

The Timing of Cleaning

I clean once a week. I try to bundle it all into one big push so I can rush through the tasks and then live in a peaceful and blissful state of ignorance for another week.

It honestly feels like Joey is cleaning *constantly*. He practically prances around the house with his cleaning supplies. Feeling a sense of satisfaction and apparent triumph each time he removes a speck of dust from a location so obscure that it would have made Queen Elizabeth's housekeeper nod in approval.

I've not even mentioned Joey's must-do-this-before-bedtime vacuum routine. Admittedly this leaves the floors gloriously clean for my bare feet every morning, but the habit still takes a good half hour before bed every night—a half hour that to me is valuable time to recharge and have fun after our son is asleep.

I suspected none of this until the moment my husband turned the corner that autumn afternoon wearing his headlamp.

The Problem of Cleaning

Although Joey explained that he didn't expect me to clean the way that he did, the next few weeks began to show something different.

I'd clean.

Then my husband would reclean.

He'd come home from a few days of traveling for work. After a few minutes, his joy would turn to mild disappointment as he saw the mess of our house. A mess that I honestly just couldn't see. Even on weekends, when I'd tried hard to deep clean—well, not "headlamp" hard, but hard for me—it still wasn't up to code. After a few months of this, we were both frustrated.

It seemed to me that Joey thought I was a messy, irresponsible slob, and I thought he was acting like a teacher who keeps telling you that you have great potential if you'd only "apply yourself."

The worst part was that the dissatisfaction we were both feeling with each other started to spread to other areas of our relationship. We began to fight about other things that seemed to pop up on the "heads up" display in front of us. Differences in how we did the laundry. How we managed the budget. Or what we watched on television. Differences in loading and unloading the dishwasher. The correct way to fold towels. And even what we were having for dinner.

Honestly, it felt like we were fighting about everything. I struggled to find one issue where we seemed to be on the same page.

Remember that chilling stat from Dr. Gottman about how so many of the problems we face are driven by fundamental differences in personality? Well, as you may understand, these differences can develop into perpetual problems—disagreements that seem to come back again and again. We feel like we can't get free of them.

This is exactly where Joey and I found ourselves. It was never *big* issues like honesty or integrity. It was a million little issues that were adding up and beginning to wreak havoc on our relationship. It was relational death by a thousand emotional paper cuts.

Before we knew it, we were six months into our marriage, and both of us were wondering what our future would look like. *Had we made a huge mistake?*

Realizing that we needed help, Joey and I set up a lunch date with our friends Mike and Jenn. Mike and Jenn had been married for three years. From our perspective, this made them newly married enough to remember the challenges but also married long enough to have worked out some of the kinks. Or so we thought.

As we sat down at one of our favorite cafés, Mike asked the question we both knew was coming: "So, how are you guys doing?"

Joey and I glanced at each other and then jumped right into it.

"I guess we are feeling really discouraged. We really love each other, but we didn't expect marriage to be this hard," Joey said, squeezing my hand.

"The worst part is, it seems like everything we are struggling with is really small," I added. "Or we keep fighting over the basics, like budgeting and paying bills. Things that we were both doing successfully before we got married."

Nodding in agreement, Joey said, "It just seems like no matter how hard we try, we can't figure out how to do these things *together*."

We anxiously waited to hear a nugget of wisdom that would solve all our problems immediately—and hopefully forever.

Their life-changing response? Our so-called friends burst into laughter. It was hysterical to them. But after a few moments of seeing us sitting there stone-faced, they stopped laughing and wiped their eyes.

That's when Jenn grabbed my hand and said with a giggle, "Welcome to the Merge, friends!"

Welcome to the Merge

Joey and I both stared at them blankly.

"The *what*?" I finally asked.

"The Merge!" Mike said with far more excitement than I felt this mysterious and seemingly unhelpful phrase deserved.

Little did I know at the time that Joey and I were about to learn more than just a new phrase to describe the beginning of a marriage. We really *were* about to get that God-given nugget of wisdom we'd been praying for from our friends.

The wisdom that our friends offered us that day would help us immensely over the next six months of our marriage. And we still use it today. It's allowed us to blend our differences into blessings, helping us nurture a more intimate relationship. And it's something we've taught couples and families across the country. And now we are honored to share that wisdom with you.

We weren't able to anticipate any of this at the time, however. That morning at the café, after she had stopped laughing, Jenn went on to say, "Marriage isn't easy. You both need to have some grace for each other."

I rolled my eyes. I didn't want to hear *that*.

"Blending your lives is a process," Jenn continued. "It's going to take time, and it's going to have ups and downs. You need to take it one small step at a time."

Her words felt like a cheese grater on my already blistered and sunburned emotions. Yet some part of me knew she was right. Real wisdom rarely starts with a quick fix. Joey and I were going to have to put in the work, grow together, and learn to adapt.

We had no idea how to actually do those things. But that conversation marked an important shift in our marriage.

Health and bonding began to replace anger and frustration, and it started with the mental picture that Jenn painted for us that day.

Jenn's picture was of two very different lives colliding like two rivers, with the resulting turbulence eventually mellowing into a single, peaceful waterway. It was an effective image for Joey and me; we immediately pictured the beautiful clashing of water at Spokane Falls in the heart of downtown Spokane, Washington, right near where Joey went to college. It's a popular place to go whitewater rafting.

If you've ever been whitewater rafting, you know that it can be lifesaving to have a guide go with you. Someone who knows the river. Knows its twists and turns. Someone who can help you avoid rough spots where you could get stuck or where your raft could turn over. And having a guide or mentor can be helpful on the journey through marriage, too. In this book, I want to be the guide that Joey and I wished we'd had during the early weeks and months of our marriage.

Maybe you're in the newlywed stage and are reading this book because you feel the way Joey and I did. Maybe you are reading this book before your wedding and are hoping to learn new strategies to make your marriage stronger before it starts. Or maybe you've been married for years and are still learning to merge your differences and grow together. No matter what stage of marriage you're in, my prayer is that we can all learn and grow together. You do not have to spend your whole married life stuck reliving those perpetual problems.

It won't be easy. However, learning how to make the Merge work better will be incredibly rewarding. And we hope that when you're done reading this, you'll share your Merge story and wisdom with other couples to help encourage them as well.

None of us are perfect, and I certainly don't have all the answers. But I do know that God has changed me through the use of the small, practical ideas this book discusses. He's changed Joey, too. And by God's grace, these ideas have helped other couples as well.

For Joey and me, learning to make the Merge has strengthened our relationship. Yes, we still have conflict, but now we have tools to help us get through those times. We have healthy processes to keep our issues manageable and our relationship strong. Most of all, we have the perspective and the faith that we can work through our issues. We know that when we fail, there is a way to repair and make our relationship stronger than it was before. We know firsthand that the Merge has strengthened us rather than destroyed us. Joey and I hope that as you read this book, this will be your experience too.

In this book, I'll often be using "we" to represent Joey and me. While I may be the one writing, I must be clear that nothing in this book would be possible without my husband. Joey has been instrumental in brainstorming, listening, and editing. He's also way better at this process of merging than I could ever be. While I sometimes think it's his name that should be on the cover, the thought of writing gives Joey hives. But his voice is here. His ideas are here. His stories are here. And his *wisdom* is here. So, from my perspective, that makes this book a "we"—not just a "me."

One other important thing to note: The advice and tools in this book are *not* designed to help if one or both of you are experiencing active addiction, extreme mental health issues, or abuse in your marriage. As someone who has lived through abuse personally, I know firsthand that no marriage book can stop abuse. And no book can stop the effects of addiction or mental health challenges. (In fact, depending on the book, it could actually increase the ability of the abuser or addict to manipulate, control, and harm.)

But there *are* resources that can help. Hope, healing, and safety are all possible for you, and for your spouse, if he or she chooses. If these situations are present in your marriage, I'd like you to do two things:

1. Get help. The National Domestic Violence Hotline at thehotline.org is a great resource. So is the Substance Abuse and Mental Health Services Administration at samhsa.gov. Focus on the Family also has resources that can help. Contact a counselor at (855) 771-4357.
2. Tell someone you trust what you are experiencing. Please know that you are not alone. If you would like to chat or share your story, I'm here to help and listen as well.

Remember, God's design for marriage never includes abuse. Or addiction. And there are helpful resources that are available, but they are not found in this book.

The Plan for Helping You Make the Merge

To help you make a successful Merge, this book is divided into four parts.

In the rest of part 1, we'll help you better understand the Merge and coach you through the process of discovering what it looks like in your marriage.

In part 2, we'll introduce five tools that can move you from conflict and chaos to connection and greater commitment. At the end of each tool, you'll find suggestions for a date night. You can use the ideas we've provided or create your own. The goal is to make sure that you are intentionally making time to better understand and apply each tool we've discussed—a tangible way of moving from information to transformation.

In part 3, you will use the five tools to create your personal Merge Map. Your Merge Map is a powerful tool that will help you navigate the Merge together. We'll also discuss the importance of Merge Mates and how they can help you maintain positive, long-term change.

Finally, part 4 will challenge you to do something great: to help one other couple currently struggling through their own Merge. Help them calm the waters by sharing some of the small things you've learned to create connection in your own marriage.

We began this chapter by sharing what may have seemed like a small, inconsequential thing: Joey wearing a headlamp. It was the moment I started to realize what the Merge was going to mean for me. But let's dig deeper into this idea of the Merge to better understand how small things really can be the things that break or bond you.

What Was Your Merge Moment?

STILL NOT SURE HOW SIGNIFICANT this concept of merging is to your marital, emotional, and spiritual health? Let's look at four couples who found themselves facing their own Merge Moments just as Joey and I did. These were moments when the challenges seemed so overwhelming that the couples wondered if their marriages would survive—moments when they felt things were so challenging that perhaps they would never be okay again.

Gavin and Brielle's Story

When Gavin and Brielle met at age eighteen, they had no idea that they had each found their future spouse. After a few years of being friends, they started dating. Soon after, they became engaged.

Gavin and Brielle took seriously the advice to do premarital counseling. They started with a church counselor, who realized after a few sessions that the couple would need some additional support because of their difficult family backgrounds. So they were referred to a second counselor, with whom they met for eighteen months.

Gavin and Brielle spent the better part of their engagement in counseling, setting expectations for their marriage and processing the dysfunction of their families together.

Going into their wedding day, they felt reasonably confident that their marriage would be smooth sailing. After all, they had already done more counseling during their engagement than the average couple does. But all too soon, the Merge appeared.

"It actually started at our wedding," Brielle shared. "Gavin's mom made it very clear that day to me, and to all our guests, that I would never be good enough for her son or ever truly be a part of their family. Prior to our wedding, I always thought she would come around. That day I realized she never would."

That rejection quickly became a source of tension in their marriage.

"Gavin wasn't vocal in his support of me or an advocate when it came to the issues with his family," Brielle explained. "And I began to let my hurt and my fear influence the way I acted around them."

At the same time, Brielle and Gavin moved in with her parents to save money for a house. After a few weeks, they realized that they weren't just dealing with the rejection and hostility from his parents but the verbal abuse and unhealthy family dynamics she grew up with as well.

"It was awful," Gavin acknowledged. "For all my parents' faults, I was always taught to cherish women. Watching her dad's outbursts of anger and his verbal abuse toward Brielle and her mom was really hard. There wasn't anything I could do to stop it. It really affected me. That was a big reason why we ended up moving out."

Even finding their own house didn't stop the issues with both sets of in-laws.

"We should have known when we got referred for 'extra counseling' that we were in for a long road ahead," Gavin joked. "But truthfully, we both felt really blindsided."

"We'd go to his parents' house, and we'd end up fighting," Brielle lamented. "Then we'd go to my parents' house, and we'd end up fighting. It was exhausting and really hard on our relationship."

As the issues with their in-laws grew, the Merge began to affect other areas of their marriage.

"We were fighting over our finances, the amount of quality time we'd spend together, and so many other things that I can't remember them all," Gavin recalled. "That was the moment we realized we were up against the merge of two broken backgrounds. It felt like we were treading water, but every direction we turned, it seemed like hundreds of miles to shore. We knew we couldn't stop treading water, and we didn't want to drown. But we were exhausted."

Micah and Chloe's Story

For Micah and Chloe, the Merge looked very different.

Micah had been married once before. He had two daughters, Emma and Brooklyn. Chloe had a son, Rowen, from a prior relationship that ended when Rowen's father became abusive. They were in their midforties, and both had been single parents for several years.

Both Micah and Chloe became Christians after their previous relationships, and they met through mutual friends who set them up. Going into their marriage, the couple knew that there would be some bumps in blending two families together. However, nothing prepared them for the Merge.

"Immediately it became clear that we needed more help," Chloe revealed. "Not only were we trying to help our kids through the transition, but we were both also struggling with the fact that we felt like we weren't getting to enjoy the newlywed season due to all the issues that kept coming up."

"She was used to parenting one way, and I had a very different way of doing things," Micah confirmed. "This was hard on both of us, and it was really hard on the kids. We were doing our best not to undermine each other, but we were really struggling to get on the same page."

"It wasn't just parenting," Chloe said, laughing. "We were both in our forties and had been doing things our own way for a very long time. We had two different ways of managing the budget, two different ways of doing chores, two different ways of planning meals for the week. For a while, we even had two different brands of peanut butter, because neither of us was willing to change what we were used to."

"We wanted to be a team. Both as a couple and as parents," Micah said. "We just couldn't figure out how to get there."

Before they knew it, the Merge was creating chaos in almost every area of their marriage.

Derek and Natalie's Story

Derek and Natalie were both in their midthirties when they separately attended the same concert. After the concert was over, they found themselves talking to a mutual friend who was in the band, and the attraction between the two was instant.

However, Derek lived in Seattle, and Natalie was leaving that night to go home to Canada. So they decided to follow each other on social media and left it at that.

About a year later, Natalie commented on one of Derek's posts. That comment led to a phone call, which led to three weeks of daily FaceTime conversations, and by the fourth week Natalie was flying down to Seattle for their first date.

"In the three weeks before our first date, we were already asking all the hard questions and having important conversations," Natalie reflected. "We both realized early on that if this relationship was to ever go anywhere, one of us would have to leave our home country for things to work. So it was important to both of us to figure out as quickly as possible if this relationship was the real thing."

After a few in-person dates and some long-distance conversations, they both realized that it was.

"After Derek proposed, I was granted a ninety-day fiancée visa. Meaning we had to be married in ninety days or I would have to go back to Canada and start the process of getting my green card all over again," Natalie explained.

To keep Natalie in the country, the two got married as quickly as possible. But as Natalie moved down from Canada and into her new home with Derek, the Merge moved in as well.

"It was a bit of a perfect storm," Natalie observed. "After we got married, I couldn't leave the United States until I was granted a travel visa. That took over a year. I couldn't go home *once* during that time to see my family or friends. The travel visa also doubled as my work visa, so I couldn't work during that time. Derek would leave for work every day, and I'd be home by myself. I struggled with the fact that I couldn't contribute to our finances, and it was hard not to feel homesick. I left my country for our relationship, and that decision really tested us."

"I was trying the best I could to be 'home' to her, but I was struggling with opening up and tearing down walls that I didn't realize were still there from my past," Derek admitted. "That combination— of her needing more from me and me wrestling with being able to give that to her—really pushed us into some uncomfortable places."

Finally, Natalie received her visa. But soon the COVID-19 lockdowns hit. Derek, a teacher, was now having to navigate online school. Natalie, a professional musician, was unemployed again and still unable to visit home.

Throw in some cultural differences, delays in Natalie's green card due to the pandemic, and a hard hit to their finances, and Derek and Natalie felt like the Merge had pushed them to their limit. Then they learned they would be having a baby soon!

Jasmine and Beau's Story

Jasmine and Beau went to rival high schools and met through mutual friends during their junior year. While they always liked each other, they didn't start dating until they were sophomores in college. They got engaged right after graduation and were married shortly thereafter.

"We were so young," Jasmine said. "We did do a lot of 'pre-merging' while we were dating. However, when we got married, everything went from theory to reality. We were no longer *talking* about how we would do things or our expectations. Now we had to actually *do* them. And [we had to] deal with what happened when our expectations weren't being met."

After a few years of marriage, as Jasmine and Beau were still working at turning theory into action, their marriage was also challenged by infertility.

"I found out when I was sixteen that I may not be able to get pregnant. While that was hard to hear at the time, I didn't realize just how hard it *really* was until we got married," Jasmine confided.

"I didn't understand the emotional part of it," Beau said. "Or the magnitude of it. I just kept thinking it [Jasmine getting pregnant] would happen. It was hard for me not to be able to do anything to fix our situation. I felt like I was failing [Jasmine] because I couldn't come up with a solution. On the other side, Jasmine felt like she was taking something away from me each month she didn't get pregnant. She was angry at the situation. And at God. But I took it like she was angry at *me*. So we were both angry—not at each other, but it always seemed to come across that way. Which made it incredibly hard for us to talk about it."

"Every time we tried to talk about it, our emotions were so raw," Jasmine recalled. "And we were so angry at ourselves and at God that it always felt like we were attacking each other. Even if that wasn't our intention."

Jasmine was surprised to see that even a married couple could lose their ability to be vulnerable with one another. "For us, that's exactly what was happening," she said.

A Familiar Struggle

For each of these couples—and for Joey and me, as well—there was a Merge Moment when it seemed like nothing would ever change.

As I interviewed these couples, I could see they had an inherent understanding of what a Merge Moment was—that first time they realized that it was hard to come together in marriage. In many cases, I didn't even have to explain the concept of the Merge to them.

Amazingly, couples just got it. Eyes lit up. Smiles and smirks were exchanged. Couples put their hands in each other's. Others laughed or let out a small sigh. Or an audible groan. They *knew*. Or they remembered. Some were currently in the middle of the Merge. Others were newly out of this stage. And a few others were looking back after more than twenty years of marriage. But no matter what stage they were in now, they all remembered going through the Merge.

Even though the concept of the Merge immediately resonates with many couples, we think that a more official definition of the Merge is important.

We define the Merge as that moment in a marriage when it becomes clear that a couple's differences threaten to drive them apart. They're trying to get on the same page, but they can't find success. They're struggling to be connected and work through challenging differences, but they can't seem to get it. Often, this is because they are stuck in some kind of cycle—going around and around again. (We'll discuss one common cycle in chapter 3.)

During the Merge, spouses often acknowledge that they need to find a new way of doing things, a new way of overcoming gridlock and patterns that are leading to resentment, hurt, and division. They know they need help to stop going in circles, to value their differences, to appreciate each other's strengths, and to build attachment and connection. They desire to bring real joy back into their relationship as they move toward the oneness they've always wanted.

The Merge Moment may come after a season of challenges, after many failed attempts at blending differences, or after struggling to combine different backgrounds. The Merge may have blindsided you, changing the dynamics of your relationship overnight. Or maybe it has been a slow boil—but now the water in the pot seems to be bubbling over.

When you find yourself facing this moment—this point of

no return where success and closeness seem all but impossible—the Merge has officially arrived in your relationship.

You now face a choice: Navigate the Merge and bond together, or allow it to push you to a place where your marriage can break. The only way out is *through*.

Hope for the Merge

Before you panic and demand a refund, I want you to know that this is all good news. Learning to navigate the Merge together is really an act of intimacy. It gives marriages a depth that can't be manufactured.

Each of the couples in this chapter has come face-to-face with the Merge, yet each couple has not only survived it but is now thriving. Don't take my word for it; here's what they have to say.

Gavin and Brielle

"We are a unit now. A united front. Gavin is an advocate for me," Brielle said.

"We've grown to love the battles because now we know *how* to fight," Gavin added, beaming. "And we [now] have a track record of winning [together]. So we can look back and have confidence that we can get through future challenges."

Micah and Chloe

"Micah and I are a team! I know that beyond a shadow of a doubt. He has my back, both in our marriage and with our kids," Chloe said.

Micah agrees. "I don't see our differences as a problem anymore," he said. "I can tell that they are making us stronger. Better people. Better parents. Better partners. We still run into [those differences], but *how* we do things now is night-and-day different from how we started."

Derek and Natalie

"He's worked and continues to work so hard to make things feel like home here for me. He's also worked hard to be vulnerable with me,"

Natalie said. "We have a truly connected friendship, and after the past few years, we know how to support each other during the good times as well as the bad."

"Not only have I been able to tear down my walls, but I've also been able to let Natalie in," Derek said. "Before, any minor suggestion of something I could improve [on] tore me apart. Now, I actually look forward to check-ins on where we are at with major issues in our marriage. I know she respects where I'm coming from, and I respect her. It's really changed how we come together. I can honestly say that not only is she my best friend but also that we really work well together as a team."

Jasmine and Beau

"Beau chose to meet me where I was at," Jasmine said. "He stopped trying to fix things and sat with me in my grief. By [his] being vulnerable with me, our emotional intimacy and connection have grown stronger and deeper than either of us thought was possible."

Beau recognizes how patience was crucial to their navigation of the Merge. "She started to give me the time I needed to process," he said. "And I began to understand that just because I didn't have the answers, [that] didn't mean I couldn't be there for her. She didn't need my words. She just needed me to be there. Emotionally and physically. That really changed things for us."

Hidden Dangers

While these are incredible victories, don't kid yourself: The Merge can absolutely take out your marriage.

Mike and Jenn, the couple who initially told Joey and me about the Merge, didn't make it. After four years of marriage, they got a divorce. While God has done much to heal and restore them both individually, it was a challenging and disheartening season for them and for those of us who love them.

How can we safeguard our own marriages and make it through the

Merge relatively unscathed? How do we get our own victory stories? We believe there are five tools that can help move you past moments of crisis—and help you successfully navigate the Merge together.

We'll get to those tools shortly, but before we do, there's something important you need to do first: You and your spouse need to officially become a team. And this starts when you give the Merge a name.

Choosing a Name

I'll never forget December 28, 2020, as long as I live.

Joey had been asked to work in Los Angeles for a few days, and he was finally headed home. And I was madder than a hornet trapped in a paper bag. Not to mention more nervous than I'd ever been in my life.

You see, four days earlier, on Christmas Eve, we were supposed to find out a massive piece of life-changing news—news we had been praying about and waiting on for what felt like forever. Christmas Eve was the day we were supposed to find out whether our in vitro fertilization (IVF) cycle had worked. We were supposed to find out if we were finally going to have a baby.

Since a potential pregnancy would still be very early and I was on more hormones than the super jacked guy at our gym, a good old-fashioned pregnancy test wouldn't give us an accurate reading. We needed lab results to know for sure.

However, in true 2020 fashion, the lab lost my blood work! And because Christmas is a holiday—and for some reason, people would rather spend their holiday surrounded by loved ones instead of drawing blood and collecting urine samples from strangers—there was no way to get new lab results until everyone was back from the break.

I really wanted the lab techs to enjoy their holiday. But after so many years of trying, I also really wanted to know if all the shots, doctor appointments, and money spent had worked. Most of all, I wanted to know if my prayers had been answered.

Because I'm super calm and never tend to overreact when I experience stress—except on days that end in *y*—Joey put one of my best friends in charge of keeping me distracted. She lives next door, and since she's basically a saint, she planned several fun things for us to do while Joey was gone. Much to Joey's relief, she even thwarted my plan to order some expensive lab equipment so I could attempt to conduct my own blood work at home.

So back to December 28 and the day I'll never forget.

No sooner had Joey returned from his business trip and walked in the door than my cell phone rang. It was a number that I had seen so often the past six months that I knew it by heart: the number for our IVF clinic.

I quickly answered the phone, putting it on speaker for Joey to hear. The nurse explained to us that the lab had miraculously found my blood work. Did we want to know the results? You can imagine our answer! And then came her words: those incredible, miraculous words confirming my pregnancy.

I remember being so happy and so excited that the rest of the conversation was pretty much a mash-up of happy tears and excited screams on my end. The Lord had answered our prayers! We were finally having a baby!

As the months passed, and my five-foot, one-inch frame slowly became the spitting image of a double-wide, it dawned on us that we needed to give our precious little miracle a name.

Naming a baby—how hard can that be? I wondered.

Very hard. Apparently, it can be very hard.

At least it was for me.

For weeks, Joey and I brainstormed, vetoed, and campaigned for various names, but we never seemed to be able to pick the right one. The weeks turned to months, and still no name.

Our families were begging us to flip a coin or pick a name out of a hat so they could at least have some form of reassurance that their grandchild was not going to be called Baby Boy Number One when he left the hospital. I actually thought that was a pretty creative name—until Joey vetoed it.

Nothing felt quite right. It just seemed so hard to name someone

I'd never met. It also felt like my first real parenting decision, one that could shape my son's entire personality and destiny in one fell swoop. To all these paralyzing thoughts, my parents and Joey replied, "Just *pick* one."

Finally, the day came when we were headed to the hospital. And we realized that we were out of time. A decision had to be made. We needed to name our son.

So we did the only thing parents in our position could do. Instead of picking one name, we picked three. One first name and two middle names. All names we loved, and all perfect for our little man.

Lincoln James Trent Stageberg.

Lincoln—or JT, as we often call him—had a name.

Now, you might be thinking, *What in the world does this cute story about your son's name have to do with the Merge? Do you just like sharing stories about your kid?*

Of course I do. But this story also has *everything* to do with the Merge. Because it's time for you and your spouse to become a team. And giving your Merge a name is where your team begins.

The Power in a Name

Time after time in Scripture, when God wanted to make or acknowledge a change in someone's character, He gave that person a new name. From Abram to Abraham. From Jacob to Israel. From Simon to Peter, the Rock.

When King Solomon had finished building the Temple, God spoke to him: "For now I have chosen and consecrated this house that my name may be there forever. My eyes and my heart will be there for all time" (2 Chronicles 7:16). It was significant that God attached His name to the Temple.

In ancient times, a person's name stood for all they were, all they could be. A new name redefined a person's future and the promises that God had for them.

Within a marriage, there's something powerful that happens when you put a name on something, particularly something that's ruining your relationship. When you name a challenge that you're facing, it puts a target on the problem's back—meaning it takes the target *off* your own back or your spouse's back. When you give the challenge a name, the two of you now have a common enemy. More importantly, this enemy isn't your spouse.

By calling what's going on "the Merge" or some other personalized name, it pushes the problem outside you and your spouse. This is a necessary step if you are going to move from fighting each other to fighting your challenges together.

A Handwritten Note

For Joey and me, giving the Merge a name—in our case, we stuck with "the Merge"—started with posting a handwritten note.

I'm a visual person, so we set out to find a way to put the Merge right in the middle of things. Somewhere we would see it all the time. In a place where we tended to spend most of our time. Consequently, we settled on the place where we had most of our Merge Moments: the kitchen.

Because we are super tech savvy and exceptionally creative, we grabbed an old, dying pen and wrote the phrase "It's not you, it's the Merge" on a large piece of scrap paper. Then we used several mismatched magnets to stick it onto our fridge. (After all, anything that's important goes on your fridge, right?)

I'm sure you can come up with a far more creative and visually appealing way to display this in your home. Looking at this phrase—ugly as it was—became our go-to way of doing something very important many times a day: seeing, resetting, and refocusing ourselves when our differences began to surface. We were constantly reminded that the Merge was what we were really up against. Not each other. And the next time we found ourselves in the heat of conflict, that made a huge difference in our attitudes and actions.

Now, you may already be thinking, *But Kari, we have so many differences right now. How does giving them a name help?* I hear your skepticism. But follow me on this for a minute.

To us, giving our conflict a name gave us a common enemy. One that wasn't Joey. Or me. Or the budget. Or even our marriage. The Merge became the problem.

That automatically put us on the same team. The team that needed to join forces to beat the Merge.

We weren't perfect at it, but it was a great place to start.

A Common Danger

There's an old saying often attributed to Aristotle: "A common danger unites even the bitterest enemies."

While I hope and pray that you and your spouse don't feel like bitter enemies, having a common enemy can indeed unite you as a couple. For Joey and me, finding an enemy outside ourselves—the Merge—brought us together. And it dramatically cut down the amount of time we were spending trying to blame each other.

This can be true for you as well. If you stay divided, you'll become overwhelmed by how big the problems seem. Or you'll just continue to attack each other instead of joining forces and taking on the Merge together.

It's so easy to just do "more of the same," which never brings change. However, if you become a team, you can navigate the Merge. Indeed, yelling "It's the Merge!" (or whatever you decide to call it) is far more satisfying to say in tough moments than "Why in the world are we having this same conversation?" Plus, it's far *less* damaging than saying, "It's your fault that we're talking about this again!"

So take this as the formal announcement: You and your spouse are now officially a team working together to defeat the Merge. You are no longer individuals taking it on alone.

That's the starting point. You've now got a name for your Merge, even if it's just "the Merge." Now you're ready to jump into learning five Merge-busting tools that can help you get past it and move into the oneness and connection you've longed for. The first Merge buster will help you stop doing something that may be damaging your relationship again and again.

Congratulations! You've named your Merge! To cement this huge decision, I'd like you to take one more small step—one that will allow Joey and me to help cheer for you and encourage you as you work your way through this book and through the Merge. Go to KariTrentStageberg.com and find the link for Making the Merge Challenge. When you sign up, you'll get five emails—one for each Merge Tool—as well as access to special videos and other encouraging resources to help you as you journey through this book and beyond. You'll learn more about Merge Mates later in this book, but for now, let Joey and me cheer for you. Sign up for free today.

PART TWO

Five Crucial Merge Tools

Your First Merge Tool:
Stopping the Mergenado

So far, we've introduced you to the concept of the Merge. And you've met several couples who have seen the Merge impact their marriages. We've also encouraged you and your spouse to give your Merge a name—to get that target off each other's back and put it where it's supposed to be: directly onto the issue that's making life so challenging! We've also asked you to sign up for our Making the Merge Challenge so we can help you along the way. That's a lot to get a hold of.

Now we are going to move from information to action. We will focus on five tools we've discovered that can greatly help couples make it through their Merge.

A Relationship-Ruining Cycle

I'm sure you've heard about the (very) bad comedy-horror movie series called *Sharknado*. If not, just Google the trailer and enjoy.

I'm going to go out on a limb and say that the best part about any of those movies—including the mockumentary spin-off *Sharknado: Heart of Sharkness*—is right there in the title. Two things most people are deathly afraid of are sharks (guaranteed to keep scaring you every day of Discovery Channel's Shark Week) and tornadoes (which are always terrible to consider or live through). Those two fears were cleverly put together to invent a brilliant new word: *Sharknado*.

This first Merge Tool borrows from that title. That's because there really are two things that couples face in making the Merge. There's the Merge itself. But there's also the Merge tornado—the destructive cycle of action and reaction that makes the Merge harder.

So we've created a term that connects these two challenging things: *the Mergenado!*

(Cue the clamor for movie rights.)

The Merge is the big, overall struggle. It's about how our differences bring us to a point where we must merge and change. But there's also something that keeps us stuck in the Merge—and prevents us from ever being able to move past it. This is the Mergenado.

Think of the tornado grabbing hold of Dorothy's house in *The Wizard of Oz* and whirling it around and around. It's a good picture of how couples get caught in a negative cycle—trying and failing, trying and failing—as they face the Merge. This negative, relationship-ruining cycle keeps couples spinning around and around, pulling them further and further away from rest, joy, and connection.

Imagine one spouse moving toward the other to try to connect on a problem or a difference. But the intensity of the pursuer's actions causes the other spouse to step back. So the pursuer gets louder, more aggressive. And the withdrawer gets quieter, stepping even further away physically and emotionally. Eventually, the pursuer gives up. And then the other person walks back.

And so the Mergenado keeps spinning. In other words, every Merge has a cycle that sucks each spouse in. And the first Merge Tool focuses on helping you understand that pattern—which comes from both of your backgrounds and personalities—so that you can escape it.

If you are struggling to make the Merge, the Mergenado *is* there. And if you aren't careful, it can keep you spinning inside the same destructive pattern for years. But you can break the cycle.

Understanding Your Mergenado

What we're asking you to do is to take a hard, careful, and truthful look at the Mergenado in your relationship. To demonstrate what this process looks like, I'll give you an example that Joey and I encountered.

As we began to look at our marriage and get serious about making the Merge with all our differences, I noticed one thing that seemed to launch the Mergenado for us right away. Whenever we started our cycle of spinning into an argument, I would immediately react like I was "in trouble," as if the situation was my fault.

Now, I know I'm not alone in trying to avoid pain or punishment. It's a common human reaction, especially for someone like me, who, in a previous relationship, had experienced painful and abusive consequences whenever I wasn't perfect—or whenever I just wore the wrong color that day. But Joey wasn't my ex. He was my best friend. My husband. My God-given gift. Yet here's what would happen.

Joey would make some super benign request like "Hey, Kari, can you unload the dishwasher?" And before I knew what was happening, I would get defensive. I found myself justifying why I had left the dishwasher full for so long. Then I'd make an argument worthy of being heard before the Supreme Court about why Joey shouldn't be upset with me. And I'd finish my closing remarks by suggesting that if Joey was so perfect and always did everything right, perhaps he should just empty the dishwasher himself.

Let's pause for a second, because I'm sure you are asking some version of *Isn't this an overreaction? He just asked you to unload the dishwasher.* And you would be right.

Stick with me on this. *Logically*, I knew that Joey was being completely reasonable. Especially since he had just cooked dinner and was looking for a place to put the dirty dishes! *Emotionally*, however, I couldn't help but feel like I had failed.

Sometimes an issue is just an issue. But when we continue to have a strong reaction to something, again and again, there is often something deeper going on. For me, this deeper reality had very little to do with the dishwasher at all. I was afraid.

I was afraid that eventually, Joey would get so sick of my failures that he'd want to leave—either emotionally distance himself or actually, physically leave.

I wasn't arguing about dishes, about putting away a few plates. I was arguing for my relational security. I was frantically trying to make sure that Joey wasn't going to bail on our marriage because I messed up.

However, all he heard was me getting defensive—and rightfully so.

It's a good thing I married a man who reminds me so much of Jesus.

But here's where the Mergenado would kick in—because it takes two people to spin.

When I'd get defensive, Joey would take a step back. He'd shut down. Get quiet. Or not want to talk at all. This is part of who he is. His personality and history are different from mine. In his home growing up, you didn't fight things out. You just took a step back when things got emotional.

But when Joey would shut down, trying to avoid further conflict, I'd get *more* defensive. Louder. After all, him stepping away was exactly what I was afraid of. So I needed to convince him not to. And then he'd step back further.

This was our Mergenado—the cycle that we desperately needed to break.

By the time Joey processed what had happened—which is what he was trying to do by stepping back—and was ready to talk about it, I already felt so rejected that it was hard for me to engage. The damage had been done.

We'd continue to go around and around and around. Always about "little things" that really weren't the issue at all. And all the while, the Merge was capturing some serious ground in our marriage.

Again, the root cause of a Mergenado usually isn't some "issue." Rather, it's a cry for connection. A need to be understood, heard, or validated.

To stop it from spinning, you both need to figure out what that emotional need is and how you can meet it together.

What Stops the Mergenado?

Dr. Sue Johnson, the founder of Emotionally Focused Therapy (EFT), observes a similar marriage dynamic, which she calls "the Tango." She presents a picture of a couple locked in a dance. That might sound positive or even romantic to some. But Dr. Johnson asks, "What if you could never get off the dance floor?"

A great question! What if you were stuck doing the same dance over and over again? As Dr. Johnson answers, if you want to change the dance, you have to change the music.[1] I like to think of the Merge this way. When the dance becomes an endless cycle, you and your spouse need to find a way to change the music. With the Merge, you must find a way to stop the Mergenado.

How do we do that? You've made a great start by putting a name on what you are facing, whether it's the Merge or some other name that you and your spouse settled on. But now it's time to slow down and have another important talk—a talk where you take an honest look at the patterns within the Mergenado that are keeping you stuck. You need to break down what the Mergenado is doing in your relationship: Identify all the parts of the Mergenado, from the event that sets it off to the final gusts of wind as the storm is ending. Doing this can help you see and bring to light how you keep getting stuck. Just like Joey and I did when we discovered our Mergenado cycle.

Let's walk through those steps right now.

1. Identify How It Starts

For us, it started with me being defensive in response to something my husband said. With you, perhaps the thing that gets the Mergenado spinning is that eye roll your spouse gives you. Or that look. That slightly-too-long sigh. That one phrase that makes your pulse quicken and your blood pressure rise.

It can be something small or even something kind of silly. But identifying what starts the Mergenado is the first step to stopping it.

2. Identify Why It Starts

Remember, often we are spinning because of a deeper reason. I was afraid that my small mistakes would lead to a big disconnect in our marriage, so Joey didn't feel safe sharing things with me. Both sides of a Mergenado can spark a lot of reactions. And knowing *why* the Mergenado begins whirling is often a big factor in knowing how to help it stop. More on that later in this chapter.

What is your *why*? Are you feeling misunderstood? Disconnected? Hurt? Afraid? Confused? Misrepresented? Attacked? Yes, sometimes a Mergenado is triggered by nothing more than an everyday disagreement. But quite often something deeper is going on. Try to determine the roots of your emotional response.

3. Recognize What You Each Do When Things Start Spinning

In our situation, I would get defensive toward Joey by trying to prove that I was good enough, to show him that I didn't need to be "in trouble" in the first place. Again, I was never actually "in trouble" at all, and there weren't going to be any unhealthy consequences even if I made a mistake. Joey never ever suggested that I wasn't a good wife or mom. Most of the time, Joey wasn't even mad. He was just trying to talk to me or make an observation. He was trying to take care of the day-to-day business of marriage and living in a house together. But I instantly reacted like our relational security was on the line and went into defense mode.

Yet Joey perceived my defensive posture as an attack. This caused him to protect himself by backing away from the encounter. Which caused me to panic, to push him toward "fixing" things. And that just made him back away even further.

So there it was, the pattern of our Mergenado. Action and reaction. Once we intentionally thought about what was causing the cycle, it all became clearly laid out for us to see.

What pattern are you both getting caught in during your Mergenado?

4. Pinpoint What Brings You out of the Cycle

Every Mergenado eventually stops spinning. In our situation, Joey would often just turn around and do whatever minor thing he had originally asked me to do—like unloading the dishwasher—and I'd leave the room fighting back tears.

What does the end of your cycle look like? Does someone give up and walk away? Do you stand there toe to toe with both of you ending up angry and defensive? Does one of you cry—which signals that it's over but that no one has really won?

It can take some work, but once you finally break down your Mergenado into these four components—describing it together verbally or in writing—you'll both begin to clearly see the specific circumstances that are keeping you from being a team, from experiencing oneness and unity moving forward.

The Damage the Mergenado Is Causing

In a moment, we'll walk through how couples can install an early-warning system to detect an incoming Mergenado. But before a couple installs that system, they must understand why such a system is important by examining the damage past Mergenadoes have already caused in their marriage. We tend to be more motivated to act when we realize what we could lose.

Joey and I recognized that the Mergenado was causing us to lose our intimacy. He was becoming afraid to talk to me. Afraid to tell me how he felt. Afraid that if he asked me to help him or do something small to make our marriage or home better, he'd experience a hostile response.

THE MERGE FOR MARRIAGE

As for me, I was afraid that I was losing Joey. But because of how I was responding to him, I actually *was* losing him, at least emotionally.

The Mergenado was damaging our intimacy. Our friendship. We were operating as wary strangers. Instead of coming to me, Joey would just "do what needed to be done" to keep life moving. Leaving me feeling alone in our relationship. Neither of us felt safe, attached, or secure in our marriage. And if we continued to live in Mergenado Alley without any type of alert siren (or ability to stop the storm before it arrived), we were going to find our marriage in a place where the Merge could collapse the walls of our relationship—destroying it entirely.

Installing Your Early-Warning System

First, since you've already named your Merge, it's also helpful to name your Mergenado. I fondly called ours "Double Trouble." I was afraid I was in trouble with my husband, which led to trouble in our relationship. Trouble times two.

Having a name for your Mergenado helps you and your spouse better identify when a storm is approaching—a bit like how you know bad weather is coming when the sky turns an ominous shade of green. Whenever one of us would begin to see warning signs that Double Trouble was about to suck us back into our old pattern, we'd speak up. Here's how that looked for us.

If Joey was the one who started to notice the warning signs, he would say something like "Kari, I'm not going anywhere, and I think you have so many incredible strengths. I also need to talk to you about something. So, if you feel like Double Trouble is about to start, let me know so I can reassure you that I'm not mad, you aren't in trouble, and I'm most certainly not going to abandon you. This is something small we can figure out together."

If it was me, I'd say something like "I know that this issue is really important, and I want to be able to talk to you about it and not get defensive. Could you help reassure me that I'm not in trouble or that there aren't any hidden consequences coming? That would really help me as we talk about this together."

Now, I realize that doing all this may not sound necessary. You may be thinking, *Who has the time to actually do that?* Or *Shouldn't we already know these things?* I agree that it can be difficult and a little awkward to slow down like this and rehearse some basic principles about your marriage, especially when you're feeling a Mergenado picking up steam.

But more of the same never brings change. And by taking thirty seconds—or less—to activate your early-warning Mergenado system, you can begin to stop the Mergenado from striking at all. For Joey and me, even if we did get sucked into our Mergenado's vortex, all it took to escape was for one of us to stop and say, "Double Trouble!" And, like it or not, one of us would smile. As you'll see in a later chapter, that small intervention of joy would show us how silly and unhelpful it was to keep arguing.

Again, we had a problem we could identify. A problem we could push outside ourselves, understand, and anticipate. And we could begin working as a team to defeat it.

While we still find ourselves caught in the Mergenado at times, I can honestly tell you that it's a rare day when we are totally caught off guard in Mergenado Alley. Breaking down our hurtful cycle—and calling it out when we saw it coming—seemed to suck so much of the negative power out of the storm!

So here's the plan: If either you or your spouse sees your Mergenado dipping out of the sky (or from your kitchen ceiling), speak up. Not in anger. Just "Hey, there's that Double Trouble thing again." Or "Look! The Mergenado! We are in it again!"

Then, after you've sounded the alarm, do what you can to reassure your spouse that the thing they are afraid of isn't going to happen here. Smile. Laugh about it. Walk over and hold your spouse's hand. And help them believe that the two of you—with God's help and grace—can truly find better ways of relating to one another. And you can! Especially if you are willing to slow down and meet the emotional needs behind the Mergenado.

One last thought on your early-warning system: It's important to know that you can't out-logic emotions. Here's what I mean by that. If you are sitting down and someone accidentally steps on your bare foot with a pointy shoe, what's your first reaction? Of course, there's the initial "Ouch!" After that might come annoyance. Or possibly even anger. But then, when the person is apologetic, we realize it was an accident. We recognize that it's not a threat or a problem. Our emotions change, and we are then able to respond to the situation appropriately. But our first reaction was still our first reaction!

It's the same with the Mergenado. When the Mergenado starts to spin, you may feel afraid, angry, or hurt. That's okay! You can't out-logic those emotions. So do your best to show grace to yourself and your spouse for that initial reaction. The power of that early-warning system is that now you can stop, look at the situation, and respond in a new way—together.

The Mountains Ahead

I know this first tool is a big one. It can be a lot to process. But it'll be tremendously helpful for your relationship when you can admit there's a Mergenado approaching. God's love for you both, and your love for each other, can break your Mergenado into pieces.

Once you've successfully set up your Mergenado warning system, you're ready for a second tool. A tool that can not only help you feel more connected to your spouse but also help you shrink any mountains—big problems created by the Merge—that you may feel are looming in front of you. We'll look at this second tool in the next chapter.

Revisiting Derek and Natalie

The next few chapters have date night suggestions featuring different couples who have faced their own Merge. Each date night activity is something you can do at home—for free or almost free. After all, making it through the Merge isn't about spending tons of money or carving out hours of time. It's about finding simple, fun ways to connect with each other and put what you are learning into action.

You don't have to do every activity, but we encourage you to at least take time to talk through the chapter and then discuss the questions together.

Okay, let's check back in with Derek and Natalie. When we first met them in chapter 2, they were struggling with their own Mergenado.

Derek was afraid that he was going to fail or let Natalie down—much like I was with Joey. So whenever an issue or a conflict would surface, he'd usually think, *I've failed!* And he would pull away, embarrassed, hurt, and ashamed.

However, Natalie, much like Joey, was just trying to talk to her spouse about something small. Something that in no way defined his worth or her love for him. But when Derek would pull back, Natalie would get angry. After all, she hadn't moved to another country, far from her friends and family, to end up alone.

The more upset she became, the more Derek would withdraw. And so on, until Natalie would just give up—at least until the next issue cropped up and their Mergenado started spinning all over again.

However, as Derek and Natalie began to closely examine this pattern, things began to change. Derek began working hard with a counselor who, with God's guidance, helped him deal with some issues from his past that were sparking the *I've failed* reaction each time Natalie shared something.

And Natalie worked hard to reassure Derek *before* she brought up an issue, and even just throughout the day, that he was doing a great job, that his worth and her love for him weren't tied to unrealistic expectations of perfection.

As Derek and Natalie both worked to stop their Mergenado and listen to that early-warning system, things changed. "As she chose to reassure me, and I got to work with counseling, I began to realize that Natalie didn't think I was a failure," Derek said. "She wasn't disappointed in me or expecting me to be perfect. I was the one who had that unrealistic expectation of myself."

When Derek began to break down his part of the cycle, it paved the way for Natalie to feel more connected to him. "All of a sudden it was like a light bulb went off," she said. "Together, not only could we have hard conversations, but we could even help each other heal. As long as we didn't find ourselves back in that cycle."

Today, Derek and Natalie are parenting an adorable little girl and working as a team better than they've done before. They are not letting the Mergenado run them around in circles.

Now it's your turn to spend some time talking about what the Mergenado looks like in your relationship.

Your Date Night

Play the game Twister with your spouse. If you don't own it, see if you can borrow it from a friend or find a used one online.

When you are done playing, take some time to answer the questions below. Once you have each answered the questions, pop some popcorn, snuggle up on the couch, and watch *Twister*, *Night of the Twisters*, or another favorite movie about heroes facing severe storms.

- How does our Mergenado start?
- Why does it start? What are the emotions, needs, or feelings behind our actions?
- What does each of us do that keeps things spinning?
- What stops the Mergenado?
- What can we do to install an early-warning system? How can we recognize a coming storm and warn each other before it starts?
- Do we need to get some more help individually or together to deal with the patterns that fuel our Mergenado?

4

Your Second Merge Tool: Making Mountains Shrink

NOW THAT YOU CAN MORE CLEARLY SEE your Mergenado cycle, let's look at how you can begin to replace the Mergenado with something you will really want in your relationship—the ability to *make mountains shrink* in your marriage.

Make mountains shrink? How is that possible? It starts when we feel like the problems the Merge has wreaked in our relationship are as big as mountains—and we then begin to recognize that these challenges are not as big as we'd believed.

Shrinking the Mountains

As I write this chapter, it's a perfect summer day in the Pacific Northwest. The kind of day that we locals endure the bone-chilling, rain-infused months of January to June to experience. The sun is shining. There's a light breeze keeping everything at a perfect temperature. Our dogs—and the neighborhood children—refuse to come inside until the sun finally goes down around ten at night.

My laptop, books, and "containers"—as Joey lovingly calls the perpetually half-finished cups of water, coffee, and Gatorade that I accumulate (and that seem to multiply) throughout the day—are spread out all over the table and chairs on the deck attached to our house. Even with a book deadline, I'm fully committed to this precious opportunity to absorb as much vitamin D as I can while the sun lasts. In the rare moments that I'm able to look up from my work, I'm beyond blessed to let my gaze travel over our backyard. That's because we have an awe-inspiring view from our backyard of Mount Rainier gallantly presiding over Tacoma like a queen on coronation day.

Towering above the skylines of Seattle, Tacoma, and the cities of the South Puget Sound, this fourteen-thousand-foot mountain is home to beautiful views, state parks, and hiking trails. But the mountain is also an active volcano housing the largest glacier on a mountain peak in the continental United States.

With its beauty and unique glacial peak, Mount Rainier is a popular destination for mountaineers and climbers during the climbing season. However, every summer, climbers are lost while trying to reach the peak or during their descent. Breathtaking as the mountain is from a distance, the climb up Mount Rainier is one of the most treacherous in the United States.

For many of us, as we look at our Merge, it can feel like we are standing at the base of a fourteen-thousand-foot mountain, facing that long, dangerous climb to the top. But what if the imposing mountain before you shrank to a small hill? What if those massive and seemingly irreconcilable differences between you and your spouse were actually things you could totally live with and even begin to love?

Yes, it's possible. Amazingly, it starts with something small.

When Something Small Changes Everything

A few days had passed since our friends had introduced the concept of the Merge to Joey and me. Their guidance was helpful, and so was the hope we discovered by having a name for what we were facing. But we also realized that we had virtually no idea what to do next!

Being the calm, easygoing one in our relationship (insert eye roll from Joey), I went right to work making a list of all the things that we needed to fix—and fix immediately. Joey, who actually *is* laid-back and easygoing, went right to work pretending like the Merge didn't exist. Believing that things would probably just fix themselves.

Clearly, this led us to a place of unity, harmony, and clear direction. *Not.* In reality, these diverging attitudes toward the Merge led us to a worse place than before.

As Joey and I wrestled with our different approaches to tackling the Merge, it seemed that one of two things could happen to our marriage: We were either going to stick together like a delicious multi-flavored popsicle, or the popsicle was going to melt like we'd left it outside on an Arizona sidewalk in the middle of July.

Recognizing this, Joey decided to implement a tool that began our process of becoming a team. We want you to learn how to use this tool in your marriage as well.

One night during dinner, about two weeks after we'd met with our friends, Joey suddenly put down his fork. If you've ever had a meal with Joey, you know this doesn't happen very often, so it immediately got my attention. He grabbed my hand, looked into my eyes, and made me a promise: "Kari, I want you to know that I'm not going anywhere," he said. "I know we are going to figure out a way through this, and no matter what, I'm going to be here. You aren't alone. We are going to get through this together."

Until he spoke those words, I had no idea how much I'd needed to hear him vocalize his commitment to our marriage. Though my parents have been married for over forty years, I had gone through an annulment in my early twenties that showed me firsthand just how fragile marriage could be. As I heard Joey's words, I began to recognize the shape of the mountain that stood before us. I realized that the abuse and infidelity I had experienced in my previous relationship had a profound impact on how urgently I felt like Joey and I needed to solve our problems—and how frustrated and fearful I became when I felt that Joey wasn't responding to a challenge as intensely as I was.

After all, I knew how damaging marital issues can become when they don't get resolved. Or what can happen when one person refuses to deal with these problems, no matter how hard the other person works to grow and change.

Joey's words calmed my fears. We really were a team, and I didn't need to fight him in order for him to take this seriously. He *was* taking this seriously. And no matter what, he was committed to figuring out a solution with me that would make our marriage work.

In this book, I emphasize the need spouses have for connection and attachment. But the basis of attachment is a deep-rooted knowledge that we are loved and that we are safe and secure in our relationship. Joey reinforced that foundation of connection and commitment for me. This allowed me to drop my fear that something would destroy our relationship. I was no longer trying to control everything, and I no longer felt like I had to do it all on my own. For the first time in our marriage, I really felt like we were a team.

That wouldn't be the only time Joey said those words to me. He said similar things when we were struggling with fertility, when we lost friends during a tough season, and on the day that we did the IVF transfer that led to the birth of our son. He still says these words during tough moments and on hard days—and on good days too.

That night we began to lay down some defenses. We sat at the dining room table and began to talk about the Merge. We didn't solve everything right then. And, despite my enthusiasm, we didn't create the 104-point master plan that I had been formulating in my head all day. But we did begin to take an honest look at our differences, and we spent some much-needed time brainstorming ways that we could join together instead of continuing to navigate the Merge alone.

Your marriage may be at a place where you've already shared some version of these words. Or maybe you're like Joey and me, and you've gotten several months into the Merge without verbalizing these thoughts yet, at least about the mountains you are currently facing. Either way, by the end of this chapter, you'll have an opportunity to say these words to each other.

There is something powerful about looking your spouse in the eye and reaffirming your attachment to him or her. It matters.

How can something as small as affirming your commitment to your marriage be significant enough to shrink the big mountains that you face today? Let's find out.

The Power of Small Things

In his popular and transformative book *Mere Christianity*, the great theologian C. S. Lewis writes, "Remember, we Christians think man lives for ever. Therefore, what really matters is those little marks or twists on the central, inside part of the soul which are going to turn it, in the long run, into a heavenly or a hellish creature."[1]

As Lewis reminds us, little decisions hold such an incredible power—the power to change the direction of our lives and our relationships. But that's not all. Lewis later states,

> Good and evil both increase at compound interest. That is why the little decisions you and I make every day are of such infinite importance. The smallest good act today is the capture of a strategic point from which, a few months later, you may be able to go on to victories you never dreamed of. An apparently trivial indulgence in lust or anger today is the loss of a ridge or railway line or bridgehead from which the enemy may launch an attack otherwise impossible.[2]

In layman's terms, Lewis is saying that we didn't end up where we are today overnight. We've made hundreds if not thousands of small decisions, each one changing our trajectory just a fraction of a degree and ultimately readjusting our course.

In our marriages, some of these many decisions are healthy and turn us toward our spouses. Some of these decisions are not wise and push us away from each other. Where we are today—personally, relationally, and spiritually—is a culmination of those many small choices. For blessing or for destruction, there is tremendous power in doing small things consistently.

But how does that work? Doesn't something like the Merge—something that seems so complicated—require a complex response? Lewis answers this for us as well:

The rule for all of us is perfectly simple. Do not waste time bothering whether you "love" your neighbour; act as if you did. As soon as we do this we find one of the great secrets. When you are behaving as if you loved someone, you will presently come to love him. If you injure someone you dislike, you will find yourself disliking him more. If you do him a good turn, you will find yourself disliking him less.[3]

While I sincerely hope you are not at a place where you dislike your spouse, Lewis's point here is powerful. The key to starting this journey of deep attachment is to begin acting on it, even in small ways. Like Joey did for me.

At StrongFamilies, the ministry I lead with my father, we call this principle the Two Degree Difference. It means investing a bit of time and effort into small, specific things. Saying the words that your spouse needs to hear. Writing a quick note. Showing up at the event that you know means a lot to your spouse. Turning off your phone. Putting down the remote. Planning a date night. Texting your spouse at work. Holding hands when you are in public.

You may be thinking, *I don't want to do anything. I want my spouse to step toward me!* Here's the reality: It takes more strength to initiate peace. This means that when your spouse is reeling from the effects of the Merge, you have an opportunity to step toward him or her. And when you do, it will even change how *you* feel about your spouse.

Actions dictate feelings—not the reverse. Small, positive actions lead to emotional changes.

On the other hand, you may be thinking, *We have a huge problem— there's no way doing something small is going to fix something so big!* I hear you. But stick with me on this. Let's say you're driving a car and find yourself veering toward the side of the road. What would happen if you yanked the steering wheel 180 degrees? Nothing good, that's for sure. You might flip the car, injuring everyone in the vehicle and perhaps people in other cars around you.

But what if you made a small correction and gently brought the car back into the lane? You would be able to continue safely on your journey.

Now think about how we respond to problems in life and in marriage. We *can* make 180-degree changes, though often they are unsustainable long-term, leaving behind a wake of pain and destruction. But if we make small, consistent changes, we are able to stick with them. We can add to them. And over time, we will discover that we've made significant changes in a steady and sustainable way.

If you want to begin shrinking the mountains you face in your Merge, you need to take action and be present for your spouse, and the Two Degree Difference can help. Later in this chapter, we'll discuss three specific ways you can do this. But before we do, we'd like to help you understand the power of small things to take down big mountains from a clinical perspective.

When Mountains Shrink

To better understand the power of small things to shrink mountains, let's look at an amazing study where a mountain actually shrank. To do that, we'll travel to the University of Virginia (UVA), where we'll drop in on a clinical study involving a real mountain—or in this case, a high hill.

Researchers at UVA devised a study to understand how people visually perceive certain tasks. They wanted to know whether there was a difference in perception when people faced a task alone versus facing the same task alongside someone they were attached to.

The researchers set up at the base of a large hill on campus and asked pairs of students passing by if they would like to participate in a study. To participate, the two students needed to have some form of relationship. They could be friends, roommates, or significant others, for example. They just couldn't be strangers.

Once researchers had their willing participants—and they had a lot (what college student doesn't want to skip class to participate in a research study?)—they had one student from each pair stand at the base of the big hill and told them they were going to have to climb the hill. Then they put a heavy backpack on each of the students, telling them that they'd have to carry it up the hill. They then asked them to indicate (using a simple gauge that measured the angle of their hands) how steep and difficult the climb would be. They discovered that when students faced the climb alone, they perceived the hill to be steeper and more difficult than it really was.

The researchers ran the test again with a small change: The student pairs would stand together, and the original climber's friend, roommate, or significant other would don a heavy backpack and put his or her hand on the first student's shoulder, indicating that the pair would climb the hill together.

Amazingly, every student who had seen the hill grow when they were asked to climb it alone now had a different experience when a friend was with them. The hill and the effort it would take to climb it now seemed to *shrink*.[4]

"Things that we have always thought of as having metaphorical value, like friendship, actually affect our physiology. Social support changes how we perceive the world and how our bodies work," said Dennis R. Proffitt, one of the authors of the study.[5]

The results of this study were so intriguing that the study was replicated at the University of Plymouth in the United Kingdom. Similar big hill. Similar estimation of the hill's difficulty by someone climbing alone. But this time, instead of having someone physically there to put a hand on the subject's shoulder, the researchers asked the student to picture in their mind someone standing next to them. Someone they were close to. Someone with a hand on their shoulder. Someone who would climb the hill with them. Someone who wasn't even there.

Although the person wasn't physically with the climber, the study showed the same results as the UVA study. When the subject was tasked with climbing the hill alone, they perceived the size of the hill and the difficulty of the task as greater than they actually were. However, when they imagined that a friend or loved one was going to climb the hill with them, their perception of that high hill *shrank*.

What causes this effect? And how can these principles help you make the Merge?

You may recognize what is going on here. God has hardwired us to be attached to others emotionally. We were not created to do life alone, and that includes facing problems and hardships. When we are attached to someone, it's like having a friend with us at the base of that big hill. We no longer see it as an insurmountable obstacle that will require more energy than we have. Instead, we see such challenges as beatable. We may even feel motivated and excited to start climbing, confident that we have what it takes to reach the top—because someone we trust has our back.

How can we each be that "high-hill person" for our spouses so that we build attachment into our marriages? How can we repair the damage if we are feeling more disconnected now than ever?

Attachment Shrinks Mountains

To truly shrink the mountains in your marriage, you need to be able to look at each other and say, "My hand is on your shoulder. No matter what mountains are ahead, I'm not taking it off." Exactly what Joey did for me.

Attachment, the second Merge Tool, is essential to helping us express these words to each other. And attachment is essential to living out these words—even in challenging moments—as we face the mountains ahead.

At its core, attachment is knowing we are safe, secure, and valued in our most important relationships. However, the Merge can disrupt attachment. It can remove the feelings of safety, security, and closeness in our marriages.

To help you make the Merge, let's look at three crucial ways to communicate to your spouse that your hand is on their shoulder. These tips may seem small, but they can have a huge impact on shrinking the mountains ahead.

In her work on bonding and attachment, clinical psychologist Dr. Sue Johnson observes that for couples to confidently say they are attached to one another, they need to have a yes answer to three powerful questions about their spouse:

1. Are you really there for me? *(When I reach out for you, do you reach back?)*
2. Do you value me? *(Am I enough?)*
3. Can I depend on you? *(Will you be there for me even when times are tough?)*[6]

Our answers to these questions determine whether we can shrink the mountains and make the Merge or whether we need to heal and repair before we can move forward together. The good news: Even if we can't answer yes to all three today, we have a clear and easy place to start.

So to help your spouse answer yes to these questions, you need to start by saying your own version of these things to him or her:

1. I'm really here for you. When you reach out, I'll reach back.
2. I value you. You are enough.
3. You can depend on me—I'll be there for you even when times are tough.

Those three statements are the things Joey said to me the evening he put down his fork and reassured me of his commitment to our marriage. Prior to hearing those words, I was afraid that when I asked for Joey to join me in facing a problem, something was going to prevent him from agreeing to do that. Either because he didn't want to or because I wasn't worth going through the Merge with.

Can you see how every fear I had was rooted in one of those three questions? But with that one conversation, Joey put his hand on my shoulder and addressed my fears head-on. And his reassurance wasn't just a one-time thing. He's said it again and again and again, in a hundred different ways. And I've done the same for him in key moments as well.

Putting a hand on a spouse's shoulder means taking an active role in reassuring them with your words and your actions that you'll do your best to say yes to those three attachment questions so that your spouse feels confident that they're not facing the mountains alone. You can do this with notes and texts to your spouse. You can do this with bright eyes and a warm smile when your spouse walks into the room. By greeting them enthusiastically when they come home. By talking quietly together—blessing each other and your relationship—before you go to bed at night. Small things done consistently go a long way toward helping your spouse be able to say, "Yes, I feel your hand on my shoulder."

Take a moment and reread those three questions rephrased below. As you do, consider whether you feel like you can answer yes to these statements in your marriage:

1. You are really there for me. When I reach out to you, you reach back.
2. You value me. I feel like I am enough for you.
3. I can depend on you. You will be there for me even when times are tough.

For many of us, just reading those questions brings up certain emotions. Feelings of love and thankfulness because we can confidently say yes to each one. Or perhaps feelings of disappointment, hurt, rejection, anger, or resentment when we respond with a no.

If you can't yet answer yes to one or more of those statements, that's okay. You aren't alone. Attachment issues are the main reason that couples end up in our coaching and counseling sessions at StrongFamilies. They're the reason people end up sitting down with a friend, counselor, or pastor to get real help.

Your answers to the three questions today need not be the everlasting story of your marriage. There are several things you can do to build attachment and even heal areas of pain or resentment. We'll dig into those ideas more at the end of this chapter and in the chapters that follow.

But first recognize that everything starts with that initial decision to express commitment to your spouse—to put your hand on his or her shoulder, confident that the two of you can make it through the Merge.

Revisiting Jasmine and Beau

When we first met Jasmine and Beau in chapter 2, the Merge was keeping them trapped in anger. As they faced the challenges of infertility, they found themselves angry at God and mad at themselves for not being able to change their circumstances.

But those feelings were coming across as anger toward *each other*, and it was destroying their intimacy. During a time when they needed to come together, they were pulling further and further apart.

But over time, Jasmine and Beau realized that even though they couldn't remove their obstacles, they could move where they stood. They couldn't force change, but they could be there for each other. They didn't have the right solutions or the right answers, but they could each have a hand on the other's shoulder—physically and metaphorically. They just needed to be present for each other.

Jasmine and Beau began to sit with each other, intimately sharing moments of pain and moments of joy. "Before I share this with you, I don't need you to fix it or give me a speech about hope," Jasmine learned to tell Beau. "Honestly, what I need is for you to listen, ask questions, and just give me a hug. Just sit in this feeling with me—and be willing to be *here* with me."

And Beau did. As the two got better at putting their hands on each other's shoulders, they began to allow God to heal their hurt, anger, and pain. While the mountain hadn't moved, they no longer saw it from the same perspective.

As they became a team, Jasmine and Beau were able to use their pain as a blessing, both within their marriage and in their relationships with others. Today, they are helping other couples who are walking through challenges with fertility. They have been a huge blessing to Joey and me. They are a powerful team, one that God is using in mighty ways to help others.

Even more amazingly, God gave them the desire of their hearts. They are now the proud adoptive parents of three beautiful little girls. (In my opinion, they are the best parents on the planet.) Seeing the joy in their home—and the way that they work as a team to parent and love their little ones—brings me to tears.

Your Date Night

Take a challenging walk together. If it's cold, snowy, or rainy, bundle up, snuggle up, and face the weather as a team. Is there a tall hill you can tackle during your walk? If so, it won't feel that steep if you're climbing it together!

As you walk, take turns answering the following questions:

- In your life before marriage, who was always there for you?
- When did you want someone to be there for you, but they weren't? How did that make you feel?

- What does "being there" look like to you? (What do you need? A hug? A good listener? Someone who will ask you questions? Be specific.)

Once you get back from your walk, put your hand on each other's shoulders and take turns saying, "When you reach out, I'll reach back. I want you to know that you are enough. I will be there for you, even when times are tough." Then spend time in prayer for your marriage, asking God that you would discover how to be there for each other.

In the coming weeks and months, keep asking your spouse how you can be present for them when you face your highest mountain together. Repeat the affirmation above. In fact, we encourage you to make this conversation a regular part of your relationship: "How can I be there for you?" or "How am I doing at being there for you?"

You can even bring your kids along for a walk later in the week and ask them these important questions too (though the first of the three questions doesn't really apply to kids). They may not have all the answers, but this opens the door for some powerful conversations and ways you can build attachment.

Our prayer is that you and your spouse find yourselves becoming a united force, ready to take on obstacles together so that they no longer have the same power over your relationship as they had before.

Your Third Merge Tool:
Merging at the Speed of Joy

As we learn about this third Merge Tool, I want you to think back to when you first started dating your spouse. For many of us, those early days were marked by constant joy. Picture the smile on your face after a good-morning text. The laughter you shared over dinner as you got to know the incredible person sitting across from you. The adventures. All the firsts. First date. First kiss. First holiday. Typically, this early season is jam-packed with joy.

Now consider the reality: For many of us, that joy tends to fade over time. We get caught up in life. Work. Busy schedules. Kids. The Merge. However, joy doesn't have to be just a fun, feel-good emotion from your past. Joy is a powerful relationship tool that we believe is absolutely overlooked in today's marriages. And its presence is crucial in making the Merge and in doing life well.

In this chapter, we'll see that this third tool has exploded in recognition within the fields of neuroscience and marriage-relationship research. And it's a tool I have a personal connection with. I first discovered it in my grandmother's life as something that kept her moving through many tough times.

A Secret Strength during Difficult Days

If there was ever someone who should have been broken, bitter, and frozen inside, it was my grandmother. For many years, she suffered from abandonment and heartbreak. When she was a child, her father spent most of his time far away from his family.

Then she had not one but two husbands walk out on her, leaving her a single mother of three boys all under the age of three (including a set of twins).

This was the 1950s. Divorce was rare. Women working to provide for their families was even more uncommon. My grandma not only worked but also became vice president of a large local bank. She was even featured on the cover of the *Wall Street Journal* for a plan she designed to help establish new banks.

Just when it seemed like things were looking up for her, rheumatoid arthritis hit her terribly hard. In just a few years, she went from being a vice president to being forced into medical retirement. She would spend the rest of her life battling immense pain. She received first-generation artificial knees and elbows, and she eventually spent the last years of her life confined to a wheelchair because walking was so difficult and painful.

Yet throughout her suffering, my grandmother modeled for me a powerful trait that can truly transform our lives and marriages.

Moving through the Merge at the Speed of Joy

My grandmother chose to do something that impacted her life and the lives of everyone she met. Despite the loss and the pain, she chose to look at each of us (and at total strangers, too) like we were incredibly important people. No matter how sick she was, or how hard things were, her eyes would always light up when she saw us. There was never any question that she was excited to see us.

That's it? Just look at someone like you're crazy about them? Well, yes.

What many top neuroscientists are discovering is that *love moves at the speed of joy.* When someone looks at you like you're really valuable, it registers in your brain as joy.

Remember the song "You Light Up My Life"? It's not just a song. Most of us don't realize that we have the power to light up our loved ones' lives every time we walk into a room. Or when we walk in the door after a long day at work. But we do. How we look at people matters.

Why does it matter so much?

Many people know that we have two sides of our brains, a right hemisphere and a left hemisphere. You've probably heard some of the related generalizations: "Right-brained" people tend to be musicians, poets, and artists, while "left-brained" people tend to be engineers, scientists, and mathematicians. But current brain science has discovered that reality is more complex. Indeed, we're all—in many ways—*both*-brained people. As one neuroscientist put it, "For the most part we all use both sides of our brains almost all the time."[1]

Think about that for a moment. While different sections of the brain do specialize in certain types of thinking and response, most of our experiences—every sight, smell, taste, touch, and sound—travel through and activate both halves of our brains.

Yes, the left side of the brain is where we make decisions and formulate theories and where we store words and memories. But before anything gets there, it's first processed on the right side of the brain—a bit like driving a car up one side of a parking lot aisle, turning left, and then heading down the next aisle at a slower speed before finding a parking spot.

So what happens on that right side? This part of our brains is where we very quickly—even more quickly than with conscious thought—process whether an experience or observation is positive in nature. This happens before those signals move on to the left side of the brain, where we analyze those observations and file them away in long-term storage.

I know what you're thinking. *Why do these brain traffic patterns matter? How does any of this relate to the Merge?*

Stay with me; we're almost there. But first, a question: Have you ever arrived at a party or social gathering and experienced feelings of acceptance and relief when you've seen someone there who really likes you? You can tell they're glad to see you even before they've spoken a word. How? Their eyes seem to light up! The look they give you says, "The party just got so much better! Look who's here! Someone wonderful just walked in!"

Our ability to register that someone is happy to see us works faster than our ability to register conscious thought, faster than we analyze and store the memory. And what a great way to remember the event! *Someone was glad to see me!* When we see that person look at us from across the room, our brains register joy and acceptance. We feel good, welcome, and even excited to be there.

Now imagine walking into another room, at another time, and seeing your spouse's face. (Just that sentence may have you wondering what reaction you'd see.) What expression would it have? What would be the first signal sent to your brain? What if, instead of anger, frustration, shame, or uncertainty, you saw joy and acceptance in your spouse's face? Just by that initial joy-filled smile, you'd know your spouse was crazy about you.

The more I learn about the science behind this, the more I think about my grandmother. Without exaggeration, every time I can remember walking into her presence—from my earliest memories until my teens when she passed away—I can't remember a time when she didn't light up with sparkling eyes, even when she was weak, sick, and in her last days at the hospital.

"The light of the eyes rejoices the heart" (Proverbs 15:30). Talk about a joy magnet! Literally every time I saw my grandmother, I felt joy radiating from her. And, biochemically, it just so happens that love and attachment move at the speed of joy.

Think back again to the picture you had of your spouse "lighting up" when he or she sees you when you get home from work, when you come back after running an errand, or when you sit across from him or her at the dinner table. Each time, joy and attachment are reflected back to you. How would that change how you feel about your relationship? How would that affect your desire to spend more time in the same room with your spouse?

Please understand that this isn't a prescription for insincerity. I'm not advising you to be like a car salesman whose eyes light up when they see you because they think it'll help them make an easy sale. Expressing joy is linked with genuine attachment—it's a reflection of authentic feelings. It's also something I've had to repeatedly practice, even though I experienced it from others.

I grew up with a grandmother and parents who looked at me countless times as if I was incredibly special. But I also spent five years in an abusive relationship during which, through words and actions, that joy was scrubbed out of my conscious mind and replaced with feelings of shame, disgust, and worthlessness.

I am incredibly grateful that even in those tough times, my parents never bailed on me. They were committed and attached to me, keeping their hands on my shoulders. And when I finally got out of the abusive relationship, I saw how important their attachment was in bringing me back to faith and love and life.

But what I've often struggled with is something you might also struggle with, especially if you've been through tough times without having any "high-hill people" in your life. It's understanding and cultivating the spirit necessary to reflect the kind of joy that radiates from who we are. Joy can become one of the most authentic parts of our identity and self, or it can be something we lose and never learn to recapture.

Reflecting Authentic Joy

I'm often amazed at how science confirms and "catches up to" the Bible's relationship advice. It shouldn't surprise me. After all, our heavenly Father, Jesus His Son, and the Holy Spirit were all there in the beginning. God made us. He created human relationships, and He knows what we need. He knows how we are wired to receive joy when we see the bright eyes and the warm smile of a loved one. His Word is designed to be for all times and for all people. "The grass withers, the flower fades, but the word of our God will stand forever" (Isaiah 40:8). God's Word, like His love, lasts forever, no matter how long it takes for humans to catch up.

But here was my problem: I knew—intellectually, at least—that my terrible season of abuse had erased many of the positives in my life. I would react like I had emotional sunburn if anyone said anything that I felt was even slightly negative. I knew there were times I reflected anything but joy when people were in my presence. But what I thought would help was more information. More education. I needed to study and learn more in order to reflect joy more. Frankly, that's what the world, even the counseling world, often tells us to do. All we need to do is get more information. The idea is that more education and more words will help you think better. And thinking better will help you change your life for the better.

But guess what? Information by itself affects only half the brain—the logical, analytical left side. And since we are designed to be both-brained people, this one-sided approach just wasn't working for me. I couldn't simply outthink my negative emotions. They had deep roots, and I'd often have automatic reactions to present circumstances based on my past hurts. I could recognize the positive things that I could do, and maybe even *should* do. But logic, reasoning, and education weren't enough to stop my impulsive responses. What I've learned—and what has been such a great help to me in making the Merge—is that we need to do more than just *know* things. We need to *experience* those things too.

Don't get me wrong. Knowing truth is important. But in the way God has wired us, it is not the left-brain information that truly changes us but rather the right-brain experiences of love, acceptance, and joy.

And those sorts of experiences are what have been the biggest change factors in our relationship. They've also led to my own growth and ability to live out joy.

So how do we experience joy? Especially in marriage?

First, it's important to remember a "both-brained" approach to the five Merge Tools in this book. Yes, learning about these tools will provide you with valuable information for building relational health. But these tools are not meant to stay on the left side of our brains! You must practice these tools with love and joy so that you can use the information and truth to bring change—to you and your loved ones.

That is exactly what I saw in my grandmother. She recognized the truth about reflecting a joyful spirit, and then she did so with love and joy. She turned head knowledge into heartfelt action. Yes, she would lie down and cry when terrible things happened to her. But I discovered she would always return to something priceless, something she discovered in God's Word.

"Weeping may tarry for the night, but joy comes with the morning" (Psalm 30:5). There's that word again. *Joy.* In God's presence "there is fullness of joy" (Psalm 16:11).

Not knowledge or more information. Joy. For my grandmother, joy wasn't based on the circumstances or challenges in front of her. Joy came from love. God's love.

I spent five years in a relationship that blocked love and faith from me like a dam blocking life-giving water from flowing down to me. The dam broke when I finally moved toward focusing on God's blessings rather than the curses of this dark world. God's love reframed and rebuilt my life, recalibrating it toward joy.

It is in God's love and blessings that one finds the ability—even when suffering from rheumatoid arthritis and having not slept most of the night—to choose to reflect joy when a granddaughter walks into the room. It is here in God's blessings that I can choose joy when

I see Joey with his headlamp on again, scrubbing at a place I would have thought was clean already. It is here in God's love that we choose joy instead of being bound by all those terrible pictures and memories stored on the left side of our brains.

Joy comes in the morning, because even through those dark nights, God's love will *be there*. Always. Ready to wipe away the tears and bring light to a new day.

A Small Choice to Add Joy

I was honored to speak at a marriage conference with my good friends Dr. Gary and Barb Rosberg. This event was for first responders and their spouses, and it was produced by an organization the Rosbergs founded called Impact Iowa's Heroes. It was an incredible event, and while there are many moments I will remember from that special time, there is one that stuck out.

One of the other speakers, Dr. Mark Mayfield, demonstrated an incredible way to build joy. He pulled out a stopwatch and had each of the couples look each other in the eye for three whole minutes. They weren't allowed to talk. And they weren't allowed to break eye contact.

The effect was powerful. Some people cried. Some laughed. Others seemed ready to start making out right there in the middle of the auditorium. Several couples shared that they felt like that was the first time they'd really connected in years. Joey and I tried it later, and the relational connection that we both felt after just three minutes was incredible.

In our fast-paced, technology-driven world, we spend so little time *really* looking at one another. In fact, that exercise initially made everyone in the auditorium feel very uncomfortable. However, the aftermath was worth every second of those awkward three minutes.

So as you get ready for your date night at the end of this chapter (spoiler alert: I'm going to ask you to do this exercise), remember that we often need to push through uncomfortable moments to get to where we'd really like to be—or at least to shake things up and get somewhere different from where we started.

So far, you've learned about three tools to help you and your spouse face the Merge. First, you learned how to name and face the Mergenado. Then you discovered how attachment to your spouse helps shrink the hills you must climb. And you've seen how joy follows when you know you are deeply, forever loved by someone. You've seen how God's love is a constant, ongoing joy generator that can give you resilience, hope, and courage to make it through the Merge.

There is another tool that's a big help in making the Merge. We'll look at that in the next chapter as we explore the choices that couples make when they begin to understand how they ever got together in the first place. (It's no accident that you're together!)

Revisiting Gavin and Brielle

When we met Gavin and Brielle in chapter 2, they were facing relationship challenges with their in-laws, a situation that was sucking the joy out of their marriage. They were also faced with a multitude of differences between their two personalities, and that threatened to do the same. What was once a fun and joyful friendship was now a hollow, and often tense, marriage. Joy was absent. The Merge was starting to win.

But then things began to change.

"We started to realize that we needed to spend time together—not just dealing with our problems, but having fun!" Brielle shared.

"We began to prioritize date nights," Gavin explained. "We put it in the budget and made it a regular thing. We never skipped a date night."

"I worked hard on being joyful, showing that in my words and actions," Brielle said. "Instead of letting the negatives impact not just my attitude but the spirit I was bringing into our marriage."

"For me, I saw that as we began to lean on God and our faith increased, so did our positive feelings about our marriage," Gavin said. "Combine that with great community, hard work, and making sure we made time to have fun together, and we started to see real changes at home."

Now it's your turn. Do something *fun* to add some immediate joy to your relationship.

Your Date Night

Start your date night by taking three minutes to build joy into your marriage. Do something small. Look at each other. Seriously. Set a timer for three minutes, and make continual eye contact with your spouse—without talking. Then take a few minutes to process what that experience was like before moving on to the activities below.

Part one: Get on the dance floor. Pull up the song "Shout" by the Isley Brothers on YouTube or Spotify. The song is just over four minutes long. So for four whole minutes, just dance together. Have fun with it! You can even include the kids in this part. If it turns into a full dance party with more than one song—even better! Give everyone a chance to pick their favorite song, and then dance things out together.

Part two: Watch videos that make you laugh. Once the kids are in bed, each of you find three online videos that really tickle your funny bone. Pull up home videos on your phone or computer. Track down your favorite movie clips, comedy clips, or creator-made videos on YouTube.

Now take time to laugh together. And as is often the case, if you find more than three videos each, keep going!

When you are done, take some time to answer the following questions:

- How has the Merge been impacting our ability to experience joy?
- Is there something we need to deal with, or give to God, that is preventing us from being joyful individually or as a couple?
- What is something small we can do this week to intentionally add joy to our marriage?

Your Fourth Merge Tool: Spotlighting Your Spouse's Strengths

YOU'VE FACED DOWN THAT MERGENADO. You're working hard to keep your hand on your loved one's shoulder. You know how crucial joy is in getting you through the Merge and helping you make wholehearted changes. All those things build on each other. As does this fourth Merge Tool: *You make the Merge by continually spotlighting your spouse's strengths.*

Turning On the Spotlight

First, we need to have an important discussion if we're serious about making the Merge. We live in a culture in which people love to talk about their strengths, and we have many opportunities to do so. Whether in job interviews, first dates, or personality tests, we are bombarded with questions about what we bring to the table. What are we good at? What results have we achieved? What value do we have?

Of course, there *are* benefits to understanding and valuing your own strengths. But there are also incredible benefits to understanding and valuing your spouse's strengths.

To be clear, it's important to remember that *understanding* and *valuing* are two very different things. You can recognize that your spouse is good at balancing the budget; you can understand that fact. But it's another thing entirely to *value* that skill, especially when your budget-minded spouse reminds you that it's not a great idea to buy that new Corvette just because it's a beautiful, shiny red and it drives really fast. (Sigh . . . yes, this is a conversation Joey and I have about once a week.)

When we start dating, we are usually attracted to a potential spouse's unique strengths. The old adage "opposites attract" is often true as well, and we find ourselves appreciating that the other person has skills that are different from our own skills.

However, after Joey and I were married—when I discovered that Joey was a clean freak and he discovered that I was not—that difference became a point of major tension in our relationship.

You probably know what I'm talking about. After a while, we no longer really admire those cute, quirky, or attractive qualities in our spouse. At best, they may be mildly annoying. At worst, they're things we intensely dislike. (Okay, the *worst* would be outright hate, but most of us are believers here, so let's just call it intense dislike.)

But whatever we're feeling, the word *value* is usually no longer on the table—and that shows up in our interactions with our spouse. When we find ourselves no longer valuing the qualities that we were once attracted to, it's very easy for our spouse to feel like we don't value or enjoy them as a person either.

What if you had a boss (like I once did) who told you, "I recognize your strengths, but they aren't the reason we hired you. So please don't use those strengths while you are here." You'd do what I did and find a new job, right?

Now, I'm not suggesting you'd ever be that brazen with your spouse. You are not in any way trying to communicate that your spouse should "just show up, do what I say, and don't think or contribute," like my former boss was telling me. But if you aren't inviting your spouse to use his or her strengths in your relationship— and then appreciating those contributions—you're essentially sending that same message.

Sure, we can be thankful that our spouse hasn't quit the relationship—like I quit the job after that conversation with my boss—but a healthy marriage does more than just not quit. A crucial part of making the Merge is ensuring that our spouse feels appreciated and valued for the strengths they bring to the relationship.

How can we find a way to stop feeling so frustrated or annoyed when our strengths collide? It starts by understanding the person God has placed in your life—and why He has done so.

You've Been Placed...

Let's first dig into a Scripture passage that you may be familiar with:

> Even so the body is not made up of one part but of many.
> Now if the foot should say, "Because I am not a hand, I do not belong to the body," it would not for that reason stop being part of the body. And if the ear should say, "Because I am not an eye, I do not belong to the body," it would not for that reason stop being part of the body. If the whole body were an eye, where would the sense of hearing be? If the whole body were an ear, where would the sense of smell be? But in fact God has placed the parts in the body, every one of them, just as he wanted them to be.
> I CORINTHIANS 12:14-18, NIV

Most of us are familiar with the first few verses because writers and pastors use this passage to remind us that each of us has a special purpose in the body of Christ. But let's focus on verse 18 for a minute, specifically the word *placed*: "But in fact God has placed the parts in the body, every one of them, just as he wanted them to be."

The word *placed* in this verse isn't just a casual term. It sounds very . . . *exact*. God placing "the parts in the body, every one of them, just as he wanted them to be" brings to my mind the care that a jeweler uses when he or she places a precious diamond in a gold ring. Or consider the precision needed to place jewels on the *ephod*, the exquisitely crafted vest that priests of ancient Israel put on before they might enter the presence of God.

I don't know if you've ever seen a jeweler work, but I have. My uncle Matt and his daughter, Kiley, are world-class jewelers. If you ever find your way to their shop in Dallas, you'll be able to watch them work. Their exactness and attention to tiny details will blow you away. And their work is something I get to look at every day—they made my engagement ring and our wedding bands.

Matt and Kiley use a high-powered magnifying glass and precision tools designed to make perfect indentations in gold or silver. Other tools are used to carefully place each precious stone in its setting so that the positioning is exact. There is nothing haphazard or careless in their work. Everything is intentional, and the end result is radiant.

In a similar way, almighty God has *placed* all the parts of the body with just as much precision, care, and intentionality. This is true of the entire body of Christ, and it's true of marriage, as well. Husbands and wives were God's idea.

I know what you're thinking. *Okay, Kari, that's all well and good. God has carefully placed us. But how can we reframe our differences so we see them as the blessings they were created to be?*

I'm so glad you asked.

There is a practical—and we think fun—way to reframe those differences. And it starts by meeting four of my favorite furry friends.

Lions, Otters, Golden Retrievers, and Beavers Can Help

Although there are many different personality assessments out there, for Joey and me, and the team at StrongFamilies, one stands out above the rest. Not just because it's incredibly helpful and powerful, but because my father, Dr. John Trent, created it. The innovation of this assessment is to connect personality types with four different animals—animals that exhibit traits that are easy to recognize and identify with. I'm biased here, but I also wholeheartedly believe that this style of assessment will best help you in your marriage. So while you can use any personality assessment out there, the StrongFamilies Connect Assessment is the one we'll be referencing here. You can take the assessment by visiting StrongFamilies.com/LOGB.

Okay, let's introduce you to some of my favorite furry friends. These animals can give us a clearer picture of our spouse's strengths so that we can begin to value those strengths—and even navigate potential areas of conflict as well.

As I go through these four animals, picture not just yourself but also your spouse. If you choose to take the Connect Assessment, you'll receive a personalized graph, but chances are you may already be able to see your spouse and yourself in one or more of the animals below.[1]

Lions

Lions like to take charge. They're assertive. They are often the boss . . . or at least they think they are.

Lions are highly motivated, quick at making decisions, and quite direct in their responses. If you really want to motivate a Lion, just tell them they can't do something. Then grab a chair and some popcorn, and watch the magic happen.

Lions don't like to stop. They might think that stoplights are a tool of the devil. They'll somehow end up in a race with everyone else on the interstate during a road trip—refusing to stop for bathroom breaks or visit the World's Largest Gumball because if they do, all the people they've passed will catch up.

There's no such thing as a problem to a Lion. Just solutions. And chances are, a Lion will be the one coming up with those solutions.

Lions aren't afraid of conflict, and they are willing to bravely take on issues and challenges that many of us would rather avoid. Lions are great people, and they're great to have in your marriage. But they aren't the only animal that's running around . . .

Otters

Otters are basically just parties waiting to happen. They know thousands of people, even if they can't remember everyone's name. This is why when Otters see you, their eyes light up, they rush across the room to hug you, and they shout out "Hey . . . you!" instead of using your actual name. But that's okay, because just as quickly, they'll buzz over to the next person they just have to say hi to, leaving laughter, joy, and probably a few headshakes in their wake.

Otters have a best *work* friend. A best *church* friend. A best *elevator* friend. And many others, perhaps just random strangers, are about to become their best *something* friends.

Otters are great at starting things . . . but not always so great at finishing them. After all, why worry about boring things like tasks and details when there are new projects to start, new experiences with friends to create, and new people to meet?

Otters are great encouragers, and they're skilled at motivating others. They are also spontaneous, outside-the-box thinkers, and they often believe rules and directions are more suggestions than instructions. In fact, most of the time Otters don't even know that there *are* rules or directions, because they threw away the handbook and the instruction manual.

Otters are also great people, and they're great to have in your marriage. But there are other animals running around as well . . .

Golden Retrievers

Golden Retrievers are loyal, caring, sensitive, and compassionate. They are excellent at finding people who are hurting, and they'll do all they can to encourage them and get others to encourage them as well.

Golden Retrievers don't care only about the task ahead but also about the people involved in the process. They want to make sure that everyone on the team is included and feels valued, not just that the project gets done.

They also tend to buy twenty boxes of Girl Scout cookies every year—not to mention the magazine subscriptions, tins of popcorn, and other unnecessary items—from the children of coworkers and extended family members. It seems to be genetically impossible for Golden Retrievers to utter that small but very important word: *No.*

While it can be hard for Golden Retrievers to say no—they really don't want to let anyone down—they sure are great at saying yes. Especially if it involves helping others or spending time with people they know, love, and feel comfortable with.

Golden Retrievers are also the kids that will send themselves to time-out when they've done something wrong—unlike Lion children, who might try to send *you* to time-out.

Golden Retrievers are great people too, and they're great to have in your marriage. But there is one last animal that could be running around your home . . .

Beavers

Beavers are detailed and precise. They are God's organized, by-the-book architects. They are the ones who actually remember to bring food to the Christmas party because it was on their list, so we love them already.

Beavers are natural problem solvers. They're organized and detail oriented. They catch the little mistakes no one else seems to see. They actually *like* to balance the checkbook. They're great at follow-through and completing complex tasks. They follow the rules. (They also wrote the rule book, so my fellow Otters and I think that gives Beavers a leg up on that particular strength.)

Beavers are also world-class at asking questions. And then, if you ask Beavers to share their advice with you, they will blow your mind with their ability to point out potential pitfalls or issues you might run into. They are also great people and great to have in your marriage.

Which One Are You?

Now that you've met all four animals, take a minute to consider who God has placed you with. Whether or not you've officially taken the Connect Assessment, I bet you can look at the various traits described above and see your strengths represented in one or more of the categories.

For Joey and me, we run the gamut. That's pretty common. Many people are a combination of two or more animals. If you haven't been able to tell, I'm a Lion-Otter, which means I often lead the way to the party. Or at least I'm really serious about the amount of fun we're going to have when we get to the party.

Joey is a mix between Lion, Golden Retriever, and Beaver. To me, this means that he's basically an overachiever. Or that he's gifted at kindly leading others while keeping track of tasks and details along the way.

What about you and your spouse? Are you a Lion-Beaver? A full-blown Otter? Are you married to a Golden Retriever? Take time to think about where you and your spouse land in these different categories.

When Your Strength Becomes a Weakness

Since you're now familiar with our four furry friends, let's understand an important truth: A strength pushed to an extreme can become a major weakness.

Yes, that means those things you are so good at—the things you pride yourself on and that others admire in you—can actually become weaknesses when pushed to an extreme, such as when you are under stress or in the midst of conflict.

Let me give you an example. As I shared above, I'm a Lion-Otter, and Joey is a Lion, Golden Retriever, and Beaver (basically the trifecta of perfection). When we were starting to go through the Merge, I'd often notice how my tone and delivery were affecting Joey as we talked about some challenge or another—meaning that when we hit a Merge Moment, I'd get more intense, more direct, and often quite loud.

While to me (and to other Lion-Otters) that kind of communication might be a sign of a good discussion, to other people—especially to Golden Retrievers—it is a sign that it's not safe to share. In fact, there were a few times when I'd say something, and I could actually see Joey *deflate*. I could tell that I'd hurt him, that he was now in a place where he didn't feel safe entering back into the conversation. In the rare cases when he'd try to respond and share how he was feeling, I'd already lined up my three-pronged argument to bat his point down and prove that my way was superior.

I wasn't hearing him. At all. And I wasn't valuing where he was coming from. Quite frankly, I don't blame him one bit for deciding not to be very transparent the next time we found ourselves in a similar situation.

When I realized this was happening, I had a choice: I could keep doing what I was doing, pushing Joey further away and never valuing what he thought or felt. Or I could change my delivery and let him know that I valued him and what he had to say.

I'm going to pause here for a moment because this choice—to bend toward your spouse or away—is something that I love about the different animal representations in the Connect Assessment. Too often there is almost a pride that arises when we read the results of a personality test. I'm "this way" or "that way." Often this pride is accompanied by a subtle resistance to change. *This is my strength. I'm a 19-Feather-Q. I'm a WXYZ. I'm a Blue Pear. The test even says so, and you already knew about this part of me when we got married. How can I change? Why would I want to change? This is who I am!*

There is absolutely nothing wrong with knowing and valuing our own strengths. But there *is* something wrong when we are unwilling to grow and change, to bend toward the Lord and toward those He has placed in our lives. Don't allow your personality type to be an excuse for staying exactly where you are. Remember this: Our greatest strength pushed to an extreme becomes a weakness.

That's why we've wired the ability to change right into the assessment. This means that if you take the Connect Assessment today, and if you're being honest, it will nail your mix of traits and the category or categories that you fall into. However, six months from now, your graph could look very different. Why? Because *you* could look very different. In fact, I hope you do! That's growth!

Take the example above. After realizing that I wasn't valuing Joey the way I should be during our Merge Moments, I worked hard to change my delivery. For the next six months I put effort into action, and while I failed more often than I would have liked, I did begin to change. After that six-month period, I took the Connect Assessment again. I was shocked to discover that my scoring in the Golden Retriever category had tripled. For me, that basically meant that I actually registered on the Golden Retriever chart instead of being completely nonexistent on it, but it was still a huge deal. And it was making a big difference in our relationship as well.

I was still a Lion-Otter. The core of who I was hadn't changed at all. But now I was more aware of Joey's feelings. Changing my delivery—a small decision to bend toward him and the Lord—was now yielding big gains in our marriage.

Much like I did, you have a choice. You can choose to say, "Well, I'm just a _____ (insert animal name). That's what the test says, and you knew that going into this." Or you can choose the path of wisdom and bend a bit toward your spouse's way of doing things.

Jesus (who I believe was the perfect blend of all four animals) did the most loving thing for people when they most needed it. And we are called to love others, especially our spouse, like Jesus did. Saying "Nah, forget it . . . I'm just going to keep being 'me'" is essentially saying "Let's forget about being Christlike."

Again, I'm not asking you to change *who* you are. After all, I'm still a Lion-Otter, and that's a great thing. But I can tell you that, whatever Lion strengths I have, I still want to see my husband engaged in our discussions. Participating. Feeling like his voice and ideas matter (because they do). It is worth every bit of effort to soften my delivery to avoid shutting him down.

As we said in chapter 4, attachment is worth it. So make the choice to bend, to recognize that a big part of making the Merge is helping each other's strengths shine.

How do we do that?

Three Places Your Spouse's Strengths Can Shine

I want to encourage you to look at three areas where it's easy to see your spouse's strengths shine. But before we look at those three areas, consider these words from Dr. Sue Johnson: "When marriages fail, it is not increasing conflict that is the cause. It is decreasing affection and emotional responsiveness. . . . Indeed, the lack of emotional responsiveness rather than the level of conflict is the best predictor of how solid a marriage will be five years into it."[2]

You don't need to be afraid of the fact that you don't agree. Or even that you may argue. Or that you need to work through things to get on the same page, as Joey and I needed to do. What you must focus on is being emotionally responsive to your spouse in those moments. Value your spouse's strengths. His or her feelings. Value the way you can solve problems together, understanding and appreciating the way your spouse sees things. And slow down in order to involve your spouse in the decision-making process.

1. Your Spouse Can Be in the Right Place to Solve Problems

I'm an Arizona Diamondbacks fan. And one of my favorite baseball memories is getting to go watch the D-backs play the first game of the 2001 World Series! We watched the remaining games at home, and the Trent household, like most families in Arizona, was cheering like crazy, especially in game seven when Luis Gonzalez batted in the game-winning, bottom-of-the-ninth run to beat the dreaded Yankees.

These days I get to watch and learn more about baseball with Joey, who has a front-row seat to many Major League Baseball games in his work as a cameraman. One thing Joey has helped me see is the importance of players getting into the right positions. Let me explain.

For infielders, getting into the best position means being in a place where their first step can be toward the ball, if need be, and then toward the base they may need to cover. Infielders are all about quick reaction. The outfielders' first step, on the other hand, is typically either to one side or the other—to the back (if the batter hits a deep fly ball) or forward (if it's a shallow fly ball or a base hit). Outfielders are all about making the calculations required to run down a ball.

Why is this baseball talk important to making the Merge in your marriage? Well, when it comes to your and your spouse's ability to solve problems, one of you may tend to be more of an infielder, while the other one is very likely an outfielder. So one of you may want to step toward the problem—reacting and trying to solve the problem right away. Meanwhile, the other person may want to take a step back—first calculating how he or she will get to the ball. Great teams, of course, have *both* sets of strengths on the field—players with lightning-quick reflexes, like a third baseman grabbing a screaming line drive, and swift outfielders who know the best way to track down a fly ball.

Lions and Otters are like infielders. They often react first and think later. Solve the problem, throw the ball, and get into position for the next step. They are also known for saying, "Just trust me, it'll work out." That phrase, or its variants, tends to immediately strike fear into the hearts of our Golden Retriever and Beaver friends. They've been on the failing end of those "trust me" moments a few too many times. So they respond with "Slow down, let's just take five minutes to think through this."

Beavers and Golden Retrievers are more like great outfielders. They tend to need some time to think through a problem. *Is this a problem I really need to solve? Are there details that impact my decision?* They're great at doing research, studying the situation before they are ready to talk about solutions. That hesitation often makes Lions and

Otters feel anxious and tense. They cry out, "What is there to know? Just make a decision and go with it!"

Now put these two different personalities into a marriage. Can you see how that push-and-pull dynamic can create issues? *Decide now!* versus *I need time to think!*

In our marriage, I'm much more of an infielder, and Joey is much more of an outfielder. I want to solve a problem quickly and just move on to the next thing. Joey needs a bit of time to process, a bit of time to gather more information before he's ready to share his ideas on how to solve the problem.

When we first got married, a problem would come up, and I'd push Joey to tell me what he was thinking. To share his ideas *right then.* After all, I wanted to know what he thought, and I was trying to make sure that we were dealing with problems together. However, Joey often felt like he needed more information. The harder I pushed him to just share his thoughts, the more he'd back away. So I'd do something that I thought would be helpful. I'd process my thoughts out loud, starting in one place and ending up somewhere completely different, often after twelve totally unconnected pit stops and a few dozen bunny trails along the way.

This drove Joey crazy. He is an internal processor, which means he was horrifically confused about how I got to step two via my verbal meanderings, not to mention how I reached my final conclusion. But he also hadn't gotten any space to gather his own thoughts about what he was feeling.

So when I'd ask him "What do you think?" after my closing remarks, he was often completely speechless. And frustrated.

So was I. When Joey didn't share his thoughts, I felt like he didn't want to connect with me. Or I assumed that he didn't want to solve the problem.

The bigger problem? The more I moved toward the ball, and the more Joey calculatingly stepped out to better predict the ball's trajectory, the more we as a team missed the ball entirely—even if the problem was an easy pop-up that we both could have caught.

So we did the only thing we knew to do. We got in touch with a couple who had been married longer—and was therefore a little wiser—and asked them for help. After our friends got done laughing at our descriptions of our challenges, they told us about something that had worked for them: the Twenty-Four-Hour Rule.

Much like us, they had found themselves struggling to make the Merge and communicate effectively about challenges they were facing. They chose a strategy. When a problem came up, they agreed to acknowledge it and then to revisit it at least twenty-four hours later. Twenty-four hours was the amount of time they determined was enough for one of them to cool down and for the other one to gather whatever information they needed to discuss the challenge. Then, when the allocated time had passed, they would sit down and talk about the problem.

So Joey and I launched this plan into action in our own marriage. Initially I hated the idea that I had to *wait* to talk about something that felt so urgent and important, but I quickly discovered two things.

First, the Twenty-Four-Hour Rule allowed me time to process a problem with my mom, sister, dad, neighbor, and good friends—as well as a few total strangers and the dog—all while giving Joey the space and time he needed to sort out his own thoughts without getting pelted with mine. Disclaimer: Not every husband or wife will be comfortable having their spouse process marriage challenges with such an extensive cast of outsiders. Talk about and agree upon what the twenty-four hours will look like.

Second, after we gave our challenges a little breathing room, Joey was much more engaged when we did sit down to talk. And I noticed that I became much clearer and more concise with what I was communicating. The time to process focused my thoughts on what was really important.

These two developments made us much more effective at solving problems. We weren't just solving problems together; we were making much better decisions as a team.

Could the Twenty-Four-Hour Rule help your marriage? If you are going to try it, follow these two suggestions:

First, work hard to wait until the appointed time to bring up the problem again. No subtle comments like "Only twelve hours until we can talk about it." As hard as it can be, really give yourselves time to think and process separately.

Second, pick a specific time to talk, and make that time a priority. Unless there's an emergency, do everything you can to keep the date. (And if there is an actual emergency, commit to another time to meet and talk.) Don't ignore the problem by making vague commitments to talk about it someday.

The time to process a problem is sacred, but so is the time to come together and talk. This approach helps the Lions and Otters—who would have preferred just tackling the issue right away—know that there will be resolution or movement at some point. And this approach also gives the Golden Retrievers and Beavers time to process, think, and gather information, which will help them feel more comfortable as they discuss the problem.

You don't have to use the Twenty-Four-Hour Rule. You could choose to bulldoze over your spouse and solve every problem quickly—with or without their input. Or you could choose to put off solving problems indefinitely—and just live with the consequences. (Though the thought of that approach causes me actual physical pain.)

Maybe, just maybe, God has placed your spouse in your life to help you solve problems. Not just more effectively but more completely as well, giving you the ability to handle ground balls or fly balls no matter where they're hit, because between the two of you, you've got things covered.

2. Your Spouse Can Help You Process New Information

Remember those special days in elementary school when the school nurse did health screenings? The teachers would form a human conveyor belt and push all the kids in your grade one by one through a series of stations where they checked your height, weight, and ability to follow basic directions. Then, when that humiliation was over, they would transfer you to a quiet room where they forced you to wear old, decrepit headphones—the same headphones your grandmother wore when she was your age—to test your hearing. Low tone. High tone. Then the imaginary tone that you always indicated you heard because you swore you saw the moderator push the button. Finally, you were shuttled into one last room, where you were given *the* test. The one that was feared above all others . . . the eye test.

Every year, some sweet, unsuspecting child would walk into the eye exam room feeling calm and confident but would soon leave in tears holding a note telling his or her parents that their child probably needed glasses—and childhood as he or she knew it was gone forever.

Don't get me wrong; glasses are great. They've helped countless people. And today there are so many options and frame choices. And what about contact lenses?

But when I was in elementary school in the nineties, glasses were a social death sentence. There were exactly two frame styles, and both were hideous. You just *knew* that the day you showed up with glasses, you were no longer going to have any friends. You'd never get asked out on a date. You were all but guaranteed to die alone. That's a lot for a fourth grader to handle.

Sure, being able to see was great. But at what cost?

I was one of those kids who emerged from the eye exam room with a note. While I managed to defy the odds and keep my friends, it was decades before I found a pair of glasses that I didn't hate—and by then I'd had LASIK surgery, so I never had to wear them anymore. Still, I handled glasses better than my dad, who, after one day of merciless mocking from his peers, chucked his pair into the canal on the way home from school—never to wear them again.

Or maybe you are like Joey, who was shocked when I asked him about his experience with this dreaded annual event. He went to a private school in Washington. Apparently he and his peers weren't subjected to the horrors of this humiliating and very public social restructuring.

But if you were like me and ended up taking a note home in fourth grade, it was for one of two reasons: You were nearsighted or farsighted.

People who are nearsighted see things clearly up close, but their vision becomes blurry as objects get farther away. People who are farsighted see close objects as a blurry mess, while objects in the distance are crystal clear. After those two diagnoses, there are different lens strengths and other factors like astigmatism to consider. These things make your eye prescription unique to you. Two people—even if they are both nearsighted or both farsighted—won't necessarily be able to switch glasses and still see clearly.

Back to your marriage. Just because you and your spouse are part of the same home, got married on the same day, and may even share many of the same strengths, it doesn't mean that the two of you see life the same way. Some people are farsighted (Beavers and Golden Retrievers), meaning we can see possibilities in the future, paths to what could be. Some of us are nearsighted (Lions and Otters), meaning we can see and understand circumstances that are happening today—and what might keep us from reaching our goals in the future.

Now mix those two traits into the same marriage, and do you see how that might cause some friction?

Even if you are both nearsighted or farsighted, you are going to have different ways of seeing and processing things. In essence, you don't have the same prescription.

So how can you begin to value the way your spouse sees things? It starts with simply remembering that your spouse isn't seeing things the same way you do. You'll need to try to temporarily "switch prescriptions." This requires a little empathy and intentionality, and that can be hard work at times.

As we exercise these prescription-switching muscles, we ask our spouse—through words and actions—to help us understand where they are coming from. "Can you clarify that for me?" "What does that look like to you?" And we need to *really* listen—rather than just listening in order to craft a response. When we're actively listening, trying to understand, we may begin to realize that our spouse isn't as off base as we once thought. We may see, in fact, that the other perspective makes a lot of sense and adds some much-needed balance to our own way of looking at different challenges.

So slow down, have a little empathy, and do your best to see life with your spouse's prescription without assuming that you and your spouse are approaching your challenges the same way.

3. Your Spouse Can Help You Make Better Decisions

The year was 2008, and the United States men's and women's 4x100-meter relay teams were both expected to win medals at the Beijing Olympics. As the teams took the track for their final qualifying races, things were looking good. Not only were they both in a great position to qualify, but it looked like they even had a chance to win the gold.

But then, in each race, it happened.

"I went to grab [the baton], and there was nothing [there]," Tyson Gay explained after the race.

For both the men's team and the women's team, the unthinkable had occurred: Each team had dropped the baton, disqualifying them from the race and preventing them from competing in the finals.

They weren't alone. Although it wasn't due to more dropped batons, for the first time in Olympic history, the United States failed to have *any* of their main relay teams—whether the 4x100, 4x200, or 4x400—qualify for the finals.[3]

But the failed baton handoffs did cause those two big losses. And it's easy to see why. The baton handoff is one of the more technical components of a relay race, relying on split-second timing, communication, and coordination while sprinting. For an Olympic sprinter, this happens quicker than most of us can blink.

The two runners must adjust their speeds long enough to pass the baton, but not for so long that it causes the next runner to lose a step as he or she gains speed. So the runner who is about to hand off the baton to a teammate needs to start *slowing down*, while the runner who is about to grab the baton and run the next leg needs to *speed up*. Ideally, their speeds match for the brief moment that the baton changes hands, and then the new runner continues to increase speed as he or she runs the next segment of the race.

Any time one person is slowing down and another is speeding up, there is the potential for them to miss each other completely and mess up the baton handoff.

Just like in a relay race, you and your spouse are often faced with situations where one of you needs to speed up before making a decision and one of you needs to slow down before making a decision. When your speeds don't match, it's easy not only to get frustrated at each other but to drop the baton completely.

Can you make every decision quickly? Sure, you can. But should you? No, not if you want them to be good decisions.

So what can you do to match your speeds so that you make better decisions together? Start by inviting your spouse in. If you're a Lion or an Otter, this means slowing down to ask what potential pitfalls your spouse sees with a decision. (It's possible you may need to ask *twice* before your spouse truly agrees to share.) And don't get defensive if your spouse spots some problems with your decision. Take feedback seriously. *Ask* and then *listen*—don't just react. For "idea people," hearing our spouse talk about problems with our brilliant idea can feel like they are poking holes in our balloon. But what if their insight will help us make the idea better and ensure that our team will succeed? What if it will keep us from experiencing pain or bigger problems down the road? Farsighted Beavers and Golden Retrievers are great at anticipating those sorts of things. And we Lions and Otters miss out when we don't ask them to tell us what they see—and then adjust our decisions to take their observations into account.

For Golden Retrievers and Beavers, making better decisions together sometimes means speeding up. Most decisions come with deadlines. Bills need to be paid, contracts and offers need to be signed, kids need to be picked up, and so on. And sometimes, no matter how much information we gather or how much research we do, it's never enough to remove the fear that we are going to make the wrong choice. But perhaps that's why God has given us someone who balances our personality. Someone who can not only face the mountain with us but also choose faith over fear for both of us—and even make sure we step out in that faith before we miss something important.

Do you see how these two distinct traits can be a powerful combination? One of you can see the potential success of a given decision and isn't afraid to take action. And one of you is able to see potential problems and make sure that you have the right information to safely move ahead.

Again, the Lord places these various traits in your life, not to defeat you, but to help you strengthen each other and your marriage for the challenges ahead.

In the next chapter, we'll examine one last tool to see how we can work to repair our relationship when it's suffered a break.

Revisiting Micah and Chloe

When we first met Micah and Chloe in chapter 2, they were struggling to unite their different parenting styles as they worked hard to bring their newly blended family together.

"It felt not only like we weren't on the same team but like we weren't even playing the same sport," Micah explained.

That's why they began to realize that if they were ever going to Merge, they needed to value the strengths they were each bringing—not just to their marriage but to their parenting as well.

"It was hard at first," Chloe admitted. "I'm much more of a Lion, and Micah is much more of a Golden Retriever. I was afraid that he would just let Rowen [her son] get away with anything. But as I chose to let Micah have a larger role in parenting Rowen, I saw a huge change—not just in our marriage, but also in my son. It was clear that he needed someone to slow down and hear him. To provide not just a rule but an explanation or a conversation with it. And Micah was exceptional at doing that."

"Honestly, my girls hadn't grown up with a lot of structure, and it was beginning to become a problem with [their] behavior and even in their attitude," Micah added. "As Chloe began to step into that side of things, we all grew. It was incredible to see."

The more they began to value and spotlight each other's strengths, the more they merged, and the more their family benefited as well.

Your Date Night

This date night requires some prep work. You'll need to read the two activities below *before* you schedule or start your date. Give yourselves time to prepare. No discussion questions this time, but make sure you do both activities, which will help you take a great first step toward shining the spotlight on your spouse's strengths.

1. Text two people who know and love your spouse. Have them send you two or three strengths that they see in your spouse. During your date night, read their answers out loud to your spouse.
2. Choose a simple object that is lying around your house, one you think represents your spouse in some way. Wrap it in fancy wrapping paper and bring it to this date night.

When your spouse opens the "gift," take a minute to share one way that you think the object represents your spouse, drawing a connection to a strength that your spouse has.

For example: As a former railroad conductor, not only does Joey love trains, but he is also fantastic at keeping the "trains" running on time in our home. Without him, we would miss every single stop along the way (and probably derail as well). So I wrapped up a toy train that belongs to our son and gave it to Joey to open as I shared that strength with him.

Joey's gift for me was a new light switch that we'd been needing to install. He told me that I "lit up" our home and that I was the power source that gave everyone energy and life.

I'll tell you this—every time I turn on a light in our home, I remember Joey's words. And Joey has officially stolen that toy train from our son. It's sitting on his nightstand, where he can see it when he wakes up and when he goes to bed.

7

Your Fifth Merge Tool:
Learning to Untie the Knot and Repair

JOEY AND I DON'T INTEND for our Merge story to sound like we've been through it all. Or to imply that we are now immune to trials or difficult days. That's not true at all. We still wrestle through many of our particular Merge challenges. We have faced conflict in some form almost every day for the past seven years. We still argue about the dishwasher. The correct way to load it. Who is going to unload it. When is it *really* full. And so on.

But dishwasher aside, Joey and I have taken huge strides in making the Merge. Thanks to God's guidance and strength, we've learned that the five Merge Tools are not just informative but truly transformative.

Yet real transformation takes time and effort. Falling down. Getting up. And, with God's strength, trying again.

None of us are going to do this journey perfectly. But as Joey and I look at the progress we've made, we recognize that a great deal of credit goes to our desire to practice this fifth Merge Tool. And we believe the same will be true for you as well.

Strong Marriages Repair

At this point, you may be thinking, *Okay, Kari, I get it. These Merge Tools are important. But you don't understand. There is real pain in our relationship. I'm hurt! He's angry! How is this process going to help with that?*

I'm glad you asked.

Strong marriages *repair*.

What in the world does that mean? Dr. Sue Johnson, who formulated and tested Emotionally Focused Therapy, explains that all couples—and most relationships in general—eventually experience a break in attachment. This means that all couples are at some point going to hurt each other. This hurt causes a "break" in the attachment bond that was previously fully connected.[1]

Stay with me here for a minute. I have a story that illustrates this. While I live in a city surrounded by water, I've only had the privilege of being on a sailboat twice. One time was actually a rescue. My kayak partner and I were unable to paddle against the strong current, and some nice sailors—a group of former frat bros now well into their sixties and having a rather "spirited" reunion—were kind enough to pick us up and take us to shore. The other time was a few years ago on Boxing Day (December 26) when one of Joey's friends, Greg, invited us to spend a day sailing with him. That day, I learned a lot about sailing. But I also discovered an incredible picture of connection. And something powerful we can do to strengthen our relationships.

As Greg taught us the basics of sailing, there were two things that quickly became apparent. First, ropes were essential to just about everything we did on the boat. Second, without our captain's expert help, we would have been in big trouble.

As we sailed around Puget Sound, blessed by incredible views of Mount Rainier, the Seattle skyline, and the surrounding mountain ranges, I noticed that one of the ropes connected to the mainsail looked a bit frayed. Being the curious person I am, I pointed it out, and I was a little surprised when Greg didn't seem concerned. I pressed further, asking him when the rope would no longer be able to hold.

Greg grabbed a pen and a piece of paper. Then he explained some complicated math formulas that sailors use to determine the breaking strength of the sailing ropes, called *sheets*. (That was the moment when I realized that if sailing required this much math, then for the sake of humanity and the safety of others, I probably shouldn't switch careers and become a sailboat captain.)

While I may not have understood the equations, I did have some questions. I asked, "What happens if you are out on the water and notice that the rope is badly damaged? Would tying some knots help keep it from breaking? Could you tie some short ropes together to replace a damaged rope?"

You would have thought I had lobsters coming out of my ears by the look I received. Greg explained that knots aren't a good way to repair a rope or attach two segments together. If you tie a knot in a rope, you'll reduce its strength by up to 50 percent. But there is an essential skill that sailors have long used as a better way to repair ropes: splicing. A splice, or an expertly repaired section of rope, typically reduces the overall strength of the rope only by about 5 to 10 percent. Repairing or joining ropes with a splice is much better than tying a bunch of knots, because knots weaken the rope too much.

It's the same with relational attachment. Picture those big hurts, the ones where we "tie a knot" to try to protect ourselves. Maybe your knot is just you and your spouse ignoring an issue, hoping it will go away, when you both know you should be working through it. Without turning toward true repair and forgiveness, that knot continues to weaken your attachment. Or maybe your knot is some sort of quick fix one of you latches on to, perhaps as a last-ditch effort to save your relationship. A promise to be better. An expensive gift.

These knots actually reduce the strength of our attachment. And under enough stress, the rope will break. You'll no longer have a single rope but two completely disconnected pieces.

Even the best of couples will hurt one another. There's no way to avoid or escape that. We are human, after all! But here's the good news: We do not have to let knots remain and weaken the rope so much that it breaks. In fact, there is something we can do to repair damaged pieces of the rope. We can not only make it whole again but actually make it stronger than before—stronger even than a splice expertly woven by a skilled sailor.

Dr. Johnson and other researchers have found that what hurts relationships in the long run is not the strains on them, or even the situations that cause breaks. *What causes couples to completely fall apart is the lack of repair.*

This is so important I'm going to state it again: It's not the fact that there is hurt or pain in your marriage that will tear you apart. What will cause the rope to break is if you choose *not* to repair it.

In fact, this process of repair is so important that researchers are finding that when couples learn to repair, they not only heal the bond—they actually *double* the strength of their connection. That's incredible! Imagine if those painful moments not only were resolved but also led to deeper connection with your spouse.

Okay, I get it. Repairing sounds like a great idea. But how do we do it?

It starts with a choice to untie the knot.

Untie the Knot

In the New Testament, the word *forgive* is sometimes a translation of the Greek word *apoluo*. Its literal meaning is something like "to set free" or "to release." The root of this word brings to mind the image of a tight knot being loosened—*of a knot being untied.*

If we are going to repair the relationship, we first need to forgive. *We need to choose to untie the knot.*

Please understand that if there is a major breach of trust in a relationship—like an affair, abuse, refusal to address mental health issues, the discovery or relapse of an addiction, or something of that nature—then there need to be big steps of behavioral change before it's possible to prioritize forgiveness or repair. Especially if the harmful behavior is still occurring. As I said in chapter 1, the advice in this book is not meant to help couples resolve issues like these. While there *is* hope and help for your marriage, that hope starts with seeking help from an expert who specializes in the challenge you are facing. So if one of these situations is the case for you, please stop reading and reach out to an expert today. If you aren't sure where to start, Focus on the Family has some great counselors and resources available to get you started (see page 14 for contact information).

Okay, that said, let's talk about untying the knot.

In the book of Matthew, we read the parable of the unforgiving servant. It starts when Peter asks Jesus, "Lord, how often will my brother sin against me, and I forgive him? As many as seven times?"

Jesus answers, "I do not say to you seven times, but seventy-seven times" (Matthew 18:21-22).

In other translations, it even reads "seventy times seven." What Jesus is saying here is, "Don't count how many times you need to do it. I'm asking you to *forgive*."

Many of us have heard these verses. Many of us have asked this question ourselves. *Seriously, God? You want me to forgive them again?*

The parable that follows this exchange gives us a powerful picture of forgiveness in action. It starts with a servant being brought before the king. The king wanted to settle all his different accounts, and this servant couldn't pay back his large debt. In fact, the debt was so large that the servant and his whole family were about to be sold in order to make good on the amount owed. But instead of selling the servant, the king showed him mercy. He canceled the debt, declaring it paid in full. That same servant then turned around and contacted someone who owed *him* money. It was a much smaller debt than what he had previously owed the king. But when the man couldn't pay, instead of showing grace, the unforgiving servant threw him into prison until the debt could be paid (Matthew 18:23-30).

I was recently in Houston at our dear friend Ryan Rush's church, Kingsland Baptist, speaking about healing after abuse. While I was there, I was so blessed to hear Ryan share a powerful sermon on this passage. Although I've read and heard this passage a million times, this time I was struck by the fact that God has forgiven *me* for more things than I can count. Or even like to admit. But so often I do what the servant did. I turn around and stay angry at others for little things they've done to me.

Here's the reality: I don't want to receive God's grace and not be able to show that same grace to others. Especially to Joey.

It can be hard at times not to remember every hurtful thing that has happened in our marriage. But the Lord is asking us to untie the knots on those, too. To not keep a record of wrongs. To allow Him to help us forgive. And with His strength, to work to repair.

In all my work with couples and individuals, I frequently see three areas where forgiveness may need to occur:

1. Forgiving others
2. Forgiving yourself
3. Forgiving God

We've talked about forgiving others. But I'd like to encourage you to do something small right now. Take a few minutes to think through the following:

1. Is there anything I need to forgive my spouse for?
2. Is there anything I need to forgive myself for?
3. Is there anything I need to forgive God for?

You may ask why I mention God here as someone we might need to forgive. While God never does wrong, we still may feel confused, hurt, or even neglected by Him as we navigate life in a broken world. Learning to untangle that pain and move forward in relationship with Him is a major part of every spiritual journey. In some ways, that process is similar to the forgiveness and healing that happens in our other relationships.

If you are really stuck on one or more of those three things, I'd encourage you to remember that forgiveness is a gift for *you*. Consider getting some help from a professional. Forgiveness is a way to move you toward freedom.

Remember those knots, how they reduce the strength of the rope up to 50 percent. Don't stay tied up in knots. Make the choice to untie the knots for yourself and your marriage today.

A Simple Process of Repair

Now that you've made the choice to untie the knot, it's time to take steps to repair your relationship with your spouse. I'd like to share a simple way to begin to repair:

1. Share (you do this).
2. Acknowledge (your spouse does this).
3. Repeat steps 1 and 2 (if needed).
4. Reaffirm (both of you do this).
5. Change (one or both if needed).

Let's walk through these steps with an example. Let's say Joey was tired, and he snapped at me because I forgot (again) to unload the dishwasher. But let's also say I was coming into the room to talk to him about a tough email I had just received. At that point, I felt the sting of his snappy comment but also the pain and emotion of the email. So I left the room upset. And Joey stayed in the kitchen mad at me—and at the dishwasher. (Or at the dishes for still being inside the dishwasher. It's always a little unclear which one is the real problem.)

That's a break. A small break, sure, but we are both hurt and a little upset. So to begin the process of repair, later that afternoon while Lincoln is taking a nap, I pull Joey aside and ask if we can talk.

Step 1: Share

Me: "Joey, when you snapped at me today, it really hurt my feelings. It just felt like your words were unusually sharp, and I wanted to talk about it before I let it bother me all day."

Step 2: Acknowledge

Joey: "I can see how that would hurt your feelings. Thank you for telling me. I'm sorry for reacting the way I did."

Me: "Thank you. I appreciate that. And I'm sorry for forgetting to unload the dishwasher again."

Step 3: Repeat Steps 1 and 2

Joey: "I don't like to keep asking, but it's hard for me to keep the ants from coming back if the sink is full of dirty dishes and I have no place to put them. It sometimes feels like you don't care about my feelings."

Me: "I didn't realize you felt that way. Thank you for telling me. You do such a great job of taking care of our house, and you worked so hard to get rid of the ants the first time. I didn't realize I was making that harder on you."

Step 4: Reaffirm

Joey: "Thank you. I appreciate you seeing that. Kari, I love you. I'm committed to you, and I'm so sorry for snapping at you today. Will you forgive me?"

Me: "Of course. Joey, I love you. I'm committed to you, and I'm sorry for not unloading the dishwasher. Will you forgive me?"

Joey: "Of course."

Step 5: Change

Me: "I'm going to put an alert in my phone so that, moving forward, I won't forget to unload the dishwasher. I know it's important to you, and I'm going to work hard to not let that happen again."

Joey: "Thank you. That means a lot. I'm going to meet with Jay this week and get some accountability for my anger. I shouldn't have snapped at you, and I'm going to work hard to change moving forward."

Me: "Thank you. I sure love you."

And then we hug. Or kiss. Or more—depending on if Lincoln is still napping or not.

Okay, I hope you can see that this is just an example. Life is usually messier than this. In fact, I daresay it's *always* messier than this. There have been times when Joey and I haven't been able to get past steps 1 and 2. We just keep circling—remember the Mergenado?—or finding new ways to hurt each other and damage the rope even further.

When that happens, we use the tools in this book. We go back to our Mergenado, and we review the questions in the date night sections. We get a Merge Mate involved (which you'll learn about in chapter 8). Or, at times, we've even done sessions with a counselor to help us move forward.

I want to be clear: This process of repair can be difficult, and it requires you both to be vulnerable. None of us do that perfectly. But when we try—when we choose to turn to our spouse even when it's hard and they choose to respond to us in a positive way—it builds attachment.

The repair process is about physically and emotionally turning to your spouse when they are hurt. You are telling them that you notice them, that you value them, and that you will be there when things get hard. This goes back to the basics of attachment, which you learned about in chapter 4. If necessary, go back to that chapter and speak the affirmations found in that date night together.

As you work to add joy through the process of repair, here are a few other suggestions to help you keep issues at the issue level, without moving toward personal attacks.

First, if you are sharing about a hurt you experienced (step 1), try to be clear and concise. For example, "When you did x, I felt y."

Do your best to stay calm and not attack or accuse your spouse. Remember, you are turning to them to repair, not put more knots in the rope.

Second, if you are responding (step 2), do your best to validate how your spouse feels. For example, "When I did *x*, it made you feel *y*. Thank you for sharing that with me." Remember that you'll get a chance to share any hurts on your side in a moment, but this is where repair begins to happen. It can also be hard and uncomfortable. Do your best to stick to validating.

Next, make sure that you apologize when you need to. Hint: If you hurt your spouse, that's a good time to apologize.

And finally, if you find yourself hurting your spouse in the same way over and over again, it's likely time to do something different and find a way to change that behavior, like Joey and I pledged to do in the example I gave earlier in this chapter. Having the strength and humility to change may be the very thing that strengthens your rope.

One last thought on this: There may be a time when you are deeply hurt or incredibly angry and don't feel like repairing at all. If that happens, remember two things. First, it's a sign of inner strength to initiate peace. Second, it takes courage and vulnerability to risk going to your spouse and attempting to repair. But the risk is worth the reward. Especially if your spouse validates your hurt or anger and reaches back to you with humility, compassion, and grace. That is where intimacy and joy thrive. That's making the Merge. That's how you strengthen the rope.

Bottom line: If you want joy to mark your relationship, repair early and often. And if you need to, get help so that you don't wake up one day holding two pieces of one very damaged—and disconnected—rope.

A High Five When You Choose to Repair

We started this chapter with the idea that these Merge Tools aren't magic or cure-all tonics. Nor do you need to do them perfectly for them to begin impacting your relationship in positive ways. Joey and

I certainly don't use these tools perfectly every time. And neither will you. But we can't encourage you enough to give this fifth tool a prominent place in your marriage. Understand that when you leave pain or hurt feelings "tied up" in a knot, it weakens your relationship. But choosing to untie the knot and repair makes your relationship stronger.

Which leads us to an interesting concept from the sports world, one that we've chosen to apply in our home: When we untie the knot and make that repair, we follow that up by high-fiving each other.

Giving your spouse a high five may seem silly or a little unortho-dox. But it's actually a great way to build joy and connection in your marriage. Just like it does on an NBA court.

I've mentioned before that as a network cameraman, Joey gets to see many of the best athletes in the world working and interacting with each other. He's noticed some interesting dynamics regarding teammates who high-five each other and those who do not.

Scientists have noticed these dynamics too. Researchers at the University of California, Berkeley, wanted to see if there was a con-nection between physical touch and the performance of NBA teams. So during an early-season game, they monitored all thirty NBA teams for twelve different types of touches—including high fives. They found that the best NBA teams at the end of the season were the ones that were always getting into tight huddles, high-fiving, and chest-bumping. They played like they trusted each other. They consistently found the best shots on offense, helped each other on defense, talked more, and, of course, won more games.

Conversely, the worst teams in the NBA barely touched and had terrible body language. As a result, they consistently made selfish, inefficient plays, and their record showed it.[2]

Yes, you could argue that maybe these players touched more *because* they were doing better. But even that doesn't negate the fact that the more they encouraged each other with positive, appropriate touch, the more joyful and connected they became as teams.

The same is true for your marriage. True, you're probably not an

NBA player. But you and your spouse *are* a team. And positive and appropriate touch not only helps us regulate our emotions but also adds joy and connection. It can truly help make you a stronger team.

Here's what I'd like you to do: Go find your spouse wherever they are in the house right now. In the kitchen. Sitting next to you on the couch. Out in the garage. Or as soon as they walk back through the door. And give them a big high five. And then try to high-five your spouse often. Did they make dinner? High five. Got the kids to bed semi–on time? High five. About to tackle a big chore or balance the budget? Preemptive high five.

I'd also like to ask you to high-five when you repair, too. Joey and I have decided that whenever we *fail* to make the Merge, or whenever one or both of us feel like we're tied up in knots, it's time to high-five. Sometimes this happens after we walk through that process of repair. Other times, it's a funny way to break up the Mergenado.

The key is, whenever we've decided to humble ourselves and *repair* so that we'll be stronger, we give each other a high five. As a reminder that we're a team that God has placed together. And as a way of reminding ourselves that repair—and untying the knots—really matters in these crazy times. And you can do the same.

Date Night: Joey and Kari

Repair can be hard. I remember one time when Joey and I just couldn't get past steps 1 and 2 of the repair process. It was getting later and later at night, and both of us were tired, angry, and feeling like we were never going to find a solution.

But this time, instead of doing what we'd normally do—stay up way too late talking and getting nowhere—we stopped. Or rather, I stopped.

I turned to Joey and grabbed his hands. Looking him in the eye, I said, "Joey, I love you. I see how upset you are about this. And I am too. I want you to know that you are enough for me. That how you feel matters. And that while we may not be able to figure out a solution tonight, I'm not going anywhere."

Yes, I know. If you've read this far, you're probably thinking, *Wait,* you *did that? Not Joey?* Yes! See, growth happens!

After that, we hugged and went to bed.

We also called a friend to get some help with that issue the next morning.

Eventually, we were able to repair. And I can honestly say that we are stronger.

But hear this: If this chapter is hard for you, or if it feels like there is just too much to repair, you can always do what I did above. Look your spouse in the eye and say, "I see you. I value you. You matter. You are enough. And I'm not going anywhere. Even if it's hard. And we are going to find a way to work through this."

Sometimes just knowing that is the step you both need to begin to heal, repair, and strengthen.

Your Date Night

This date night will require just a little bit of preparation, so make sure you read ahead before you plan.

Each of you will prepare two things to give your spouse. Keep your items secret until the moment arrives!

First, find a picture that represents a favorite memory you have of your spouse. Spend $0.45 or whatever at Walgreens or Costco or wherever to print a copy of that photo and bring it to this date night.

Next, pick up your spouse's favorite snack from the grocery store, and bring it with you to date night. For example, mine is apples and peanut butter, and Joey's is chips and salsa.

Start date night by presenting your spouse with their favorite snack. Then enjoy some time eating together. Add your favorite romantic playlist for some extra mood-boosting fun.

Then take turns sharing about the picture you chose. Give the picture to your spouse and explain why you like it. What it reminds you of. Why it means something to you. And so on. (Bonus: Give each other a high five after one of you shares.)

Now take some time to answer the following questions:

1. Is there anything we need to repair in our marriage?
2. Are there any knots we need to untie?
3. Do we think we are in a place to walk through one area of repair?

If you aren't in that place tonight, that's okay! Wrap up date night by taking turns looking each other in the eye and saying the following: "I see you. You are enough. And I'm going to be here, even when things are hard." (Yes, you said this during a previous date night, but repetition is a good thing—and these words matter!)

If you are ready to try to repair, then pick one *small* issue to discuss together. Both of you need to agree on the issue. And it needs to be small—don't talk about the biggest fight you've ever had. Or something that brings up a lot of emotional hurt. Choose a little thing. Like in the example with Joey and me in this chapter.

Then walk through the five steps of repair:

1. Share (you do this).
2. Acknowledge (your spouse does this).
3. Repeat steps 1 and 2 (if needed).
4. Reaffirm (both of you do this).
5. Change (one or both if needed).

When you are done, answer the following questions:

- How did that feel?
- Do we need to get some more help to really repair this issue? (Make sure to get that help if needed.)

Then close out date night by taking turns looking each other in the eye and once again saying the following: "I see you. You are enough. And I'm going to be here, even when things are hard."

PART THREE

Your Merge Mates
and Merge Map

8

Adding Merge Mates to Your Journey

As a member of the varsity cheer squad, I was *technically* an athlete in high school. Okay, I'm going to stop you right there and quickly address the eye rolls and objections that may be springing up in your mind. Unless you've ever been launched twenty feet into the air, tumbled into a teammate's arms like a maniac, and finished with a double-twist cradle dismount, you probably don't think cheerleading is a sport. That's fine. We can agree to disagree on this. (I also must confess that I didn't do any of those acrobatic things because I was a "base," not a "flyer," but you get my point. #endrant.)

As cheerleaders, we trained and conditioned nonstop to compete at the state and national levels. And I'm proud to say that we won at both levels of competition my senior year. Then, in college, I was on a dance team, lifted weights, worked out consistently, joined the Beach Rollerblading Club (yes, it was as cool as it sounds), and even played on a powder-puff football team.

It might sound like I'm doing the ol' "when I was young and in shape" thing, but . . . well, actually, I am. (Those of you who've given birth to one or more babies have probably reveled in the glory of your former body, reminiscing about the abundance of time you previously had to keep it that way. But I digress . . .)

The point is, I've been an active person for much of my life. But there was always one activity that, no matter how hard I tried, I never enjoyed: running.

Well, running without a purpose, at least. If the situation was, say, running to get away from danger, or running a play in flag football, or running to the taco restaurant, I was in. But if it was "let's go for a run" just to run, I really wasn't interested. From childhood to adulthood, I've disliked running so much that I could come up with an impressive variety of creative excuses to avoid it.

But for many people I know, running is a pleasurable and endorphin-giving pastime. They bound along effortlessly like happy little gazelles on a perfect, predator-free day in the Serengeti. It also helps that, with their eating habits, lack of kids, and ability to get a full night's sleep, these particular people kind of *look* like gazelles.

For me, running looks more like primal panic than happy pastime. Instead of grace, beauty, and light perspiration glistening on my wrinkle-free and fully rested face, I end up looking like I fell into a lake and then stumbled around in the woods for a while, emerging back into civilization horrifically out of breath and begging for water from strangers.

So that's why the events of January 20, 2013, were so shocking. Somehow, my carefully maintained barricade was breached. I found myself standing at the starting line of my first and only half-marathon. I even ran into my old high school PE teacher at the finish line. He laughed until he cried and demanded to see photographic proof that I had run the entire race and not just the last fifty yards.

Clearly, the only thing that could have pushed me to such a moment of temporary insanity was a boy. Six months before that fateful day, a group of friends had persuaded me to run this crazy event. Normally, I would have laughed and told them I'd rather have a root canal without anesthesia. But this time I figured, *How hard can it really be? Especially if I might get to do some training runs with that boy I like.*

Soon I was committed. Money for the Rock 'n' Roll Arizona Half-Marathon: paid. Plane ticket to Phoenix: purchased.

I found myself stuck, realizing that there was no way out of my commitment. I also realized that given my specific running "style" (see above), trying to run with a guy I liked was a horrible idea.

Even as the hope of that relationship fizzled away, I was still locked into my terrible decision. Somehow, I needed to figure out how to turn my usual stagger-through-a-quarter-mile self into someone who could find a way to crawl or be pushed (I'm not picky) across a finish line thirteen miles later.

Which is why I called the one person I know who has completed more half-marathons and full marathons than I can count . . . my dad.

After he recovered from shock, he told me two things that immediately made me feel better. The first was that he'd love to run the race with me. The second was that since we were going to be doing most of our training runs separately—we lived in two different states—I needed to get the best book on the planet for first-time marathoners, *The Run-Walk-Run Method* by Jeff Galloway.

Just seeing the word *walk* in the title gave me a little bit of hope. I immediately got a copy of the book and found myself learning from an Olympic distance runner who told me, and the millions of others who have read his book, to start out running for just *one* minute. Then walk for one minute. Then run a minute, and so on. As I read that book, I thought to myself, *One minute . . . I can do that.*

It might have been all that I could do, but I could do it.

So I did it. Soon I was easily running a minute around the block. And then I slowly started adding minutes. Two minutes. Three minutes. And so on. But no matter how many minutes I added, I always got to keep that much-needed, highly anticipated minute of rest afterward.

A few weeks after starting my training, I ran my first 5K. And then my first 10K. Finally, I flew to Arizona to run my first ten miles with my dad along the beautiful banks of the Arizona Canal. As we wove our way through the neighborhood where he grew up, I got to learn more about his childhood. He told me stories about friends who had once lived in the houses we were passing and the experiences they had shared together. It's a run I'll always remember, my dad speaking in his steady rhythm, me panting to catch my breath. Both of us running for several minutes, walking for one minute—sticking to the plan until the very end.

After that run, there were only a few weeks left until race day. With some big projects at work and some weather changes in Tacoma, I'd still never run the full 13.1 miles as the day of the race arrived.

The morning of the race, as my dad and I stood in our assigned "corral" (a roped-in part of the road) with a thousand other runners, I could feel my nerves kicking in. Finally, after seven thousand of our new best friends started the race before us—there would be seven thousand or so after us, as well—it was our turn to run. The countdown began, and my dad and I and about a thousand other runners (slowly) took off through downtown Phoenix toward the finish line at Arizona State University, 13.1 miles away.

And that's when the music started.

G'day, Mate

At the first mile marker of the Rock 'n' Roll Half-Marathon, one of their signature experiences takes place. You hear it long before you see it. As you get closer, you realize that you are hearing a rock band— playing what often sounds like very off-key rock music.

Imagine a group of people who always wanted to be in a real rock band, people who had their own garage bands before neighbors threw them out of the neighborhood or at least filed noise complaints and threatened to hide the musical instruments. But these bandmates were determined. Undaunted. They just knew that things would turn around for them—that they'd finally get a recording contract if they signed up to play loudly (for no pay) for thousands of marathon runners.

Not that I could do any better. I'm not sure race organizers would even allow me to play. However, when you hear the name of the event—the Rock 'n' Roll Marathon—you might logically assume that they've maybe held an audition or two before agreeing to let the group play.

Having run the Rock 'n' Roll many times before, my dad quipped, "They're so bad, it makes you want to speed up just to get by, doesn't it?" True! And sure enough, every other mile or so, as we came in range of another subpar rock band, we were picking up our pace to get past the noise, even while trying to figure out what song the group was attempting to perform.

But that wasn't all. At the even mile markers, there were those athletes I talked about earlier—local high school cheerleading squads that we really did appreciate! They were all decked out in their homecoming-football-game best. Stunting, dancing, yelling, and cheering for us all. That caused us to pick up our pace too, but for a much better reason.

And finally, toward the last few miles, I noticed something else. Small groups, and then larger groups, and later hundreds, and then literally thousands of friends and family members of runners lined the course. Some would pick out random race numbers and scream for the runners to keep going. Others were just cheering wildly for people like us who were trundling by. Although they didn't know us, they encouraged us while they waited for their own loved ones to stumble into sight.

And then, just when I was about to ask the lady with the jogging stroller if she would give me a ride, it was over.

I was carried to the finish line by people the Aussies would call "mates," people who all wanted to see us finish well—my dad, other runners, cheerleaders, fans, friends, and volunteers handing out water. Even the music enthusiasts along the way. All of them helped me get across the finish line. In fact, there wasn't a moment on that course when I was alone, when I wasn't being encouraged to keep going.

That's a long preamble to bring us to the last bit of advice to help you make the Merge, which is to find a group of Merge Mates. I hope you can sense the fun, optimism, and endurance that these people give you as they pull for you and cheer you on. Hebrews 11 (and the first part of Hebrews 12) is often called the "hall of faith." Here we learn about the "great cloud of witnesses" that have come before us and surround us now as we run the race of finishing well for Christ. What an encouragement to know that so many legendary believers from God's Word are standing at the top of the highest hill and at the last mile, cheering us on!

Joey and I would like to be there with you too. That's a big goal of this book. Whenever you are just about ready to quit—you can imagine us there with you. Telling you that you can do it, that you're not alone. Waving our race medal to show you that it can be done, and that you've got two Merge Mates who are with you now in spirit. Your medal will be waiting for you up ahead!

And now it's your turn to start building a group of Merge Mates. Because you do not want the agony and burden of trying to run through the Merge alone. Because being alone is far too often a death sentence for relationships.

Not convinced yet? Read on.

Loneliness Can Keep You from Ever Making the Merge

When Ben and Jenna got married, they had a thriving community of friends and family around them. Then, a few months into their marriage, Jenna unexpectedly got offered an incredible job promotion. Along with a significant salary increase, this promotion also meant that the two would need to relocate from California to New Jersey. Ben worked remotely, so aside from leaving friends and family, the move seemed like a great opportunity. As they packed up their small, one-bedroom apartment, they laughed and daydreamed together about the new and exciting adventures they would have as a couple.

But three months after they settled in New Jersey, the COVID-19 pandemic arrived, and everything began to change. They saw their world move from "let's build relationships" to "let's lock ourselves inside." They were unable to attend church, and watching the service online didn't help them build any relationships. They couldn't go to work in person. And they couldn't even fly home to see family. Ben's dad had recently completed chemotherapy treatments, and they didn't want to risk him getting sick. But at least Ben and Jenna had each other.

The situation seemed like a good one at first. They started a few hobbies, perfected their sourdough starter, and played most every two-person board game that Amazon had to offer. They joined TikTok. Quit TikTok. And caught up on all their favorite television shows.

However, after a few months, Ben and Jenna found themselves facing both COVID-19 and the Merge—at the same time.

With the strict lockdown policies in New Jersey, they were unable to leave their apartment other than for brief trips to the grocery store and maybe a quick early-morning run. Except for those brief breaks, they were together all the time. And that's when their differences really began to surface.

I won't go into all the studies that reveal how destructive the COVID-19 lockdowns and the resulting isolation were to relationships. You've likely heard about many of these consequences, particularly for children and the elderly. But youngish people like Ben and Jenna have suffered severe consequences as well. Here are just a few highlights (lowlights?) from the news.

A *Forbes* article titled "The High Cost of Loneliness: The Other Price Older Americans Are Paying for Covid-19" revealed the incredible number of older people who, through isolation, have experienced severe physical and mental breakdowns.[1] A broader-focused (but no less chilling) exposé at the *Wall Street Journal* ("What Covid-19 Taught Us about the High Cost of Isolation") showed the mental devastation of older age groups due to the lockdowns.[2] You'll find another dis-heartening read in *Harvard Magazine*'s "The Loneliness Pandemic," an article that details how every age group, children included, has suffered from a lack of connection during the pandemic.[3]

Going back to Ben and Jenna. Even as restrictions began to lift, the only social groups they could find were all still virtual. And Zoom meetings just weren't working while they struggled to meet people and make new friends. As they were trying to deal with the anxiety and fear of the unknown around them, Ben lost his job. They had been counting on his income, and the immediate financial stress quickly became relational stress as well. Soon they weren't fighting only about small things but about pretty much everything.

"At first I thought that having it just be us meant that we would get to skip some of the struggles that other couples have faced in their first year of marriage," Jenna explained. "But with only each other and no friends or family nearby, it created an unhealthy dynamic in our marriage. I was expecting Ben to take the place of my parents, my sisters, my friends, and all my other social outlets combined. And Ben was expecting me to do the same. Not only that, but we both began to look at each other as our sole source of happiness and connection—something that we were never designed to be to one another."

While the pandemic and the move across the country played a big part in heightening these issues for Ben and Jenna, the "be my every-thing" expectation has been attacking marriages since long before the pandemic began shutting down everyone's relational outlets.

While it's easy to blame the Hallmark Channel, romance novels, or inflation—it's tempting to blame everything on that, I think—the truth is that God created us all for connection, but we are living in a society that is more disconnected than ever before.

Loneliness impacts our society in many profound ways. Anxiety. Anger. Depression. But within a marriage, the impact is different. As married couples, we generally have a greater expectation of love and connection, but at the same time, the number of other close relationships we have tends to decrease. This puts extra relational pressure on the marriage.

That means many of us are like Ben and Jenna. We are not only looking for love but also expecting our spouse to be our parent, sibling, best friend, coworker, counselor, fitness instructor, mentor, grandparent, and more. These heightened expectations can set us up for disappointment—and even disaster if we aren't careful. Like Jenna shared above, our spouse was never created to be the sole provider for all our emotional and relational needs. That's too much pressure to put on our spouse, especially when they are going to fall short.

To alleviate that burden, we need to intentionally be part of a community. How do you do that, especially in a world that is as isolated and disconnected as ours?

Three Ways to Build a Team of Merge Mates

John Adams once reportedly said, "Facts are stubborn things."[4] It's true. We can ignore truths for only so long before reality smacks us in the face. So I'm not going to try any harder to prove to you why you shouldn't run the marathon that is marriage—or try to make the Merge—on your own. The fact is that loneliness kills relationships. The wolf loves lone sheep. Lone couples, too.

You may be struggling, like most couples are today, to reconnect with or build connection within a community. Here are three pieces of advice that can help you nail this important challenge.

1. It Takes Intentionality to Build Community

There are so many challenges out there today. Not the least of which is the tendency we have to live out a terrible (in its outcome) and self-fulfilling proverb: "Do you see a man who is wise in his own eyes? There is more hope for a fool than for him" (Proverbs 26:12).

Who is the man looking to here? Himself. His own insight and knowledge. His own reality. In fact, he doesn't want to look at others at all because he is confident that he alone has the answers. This verse is a way of laying bare a man whose pride makes him unwilling to look to anyone other than himself.

This sets us up for the next verse: "The sluggard says, 'There is a lion in the road!'" (Proverbs 26:13).

It's so easy to magnify problems and challenges. Not convinced? Look where this verse takes us. The slothful person magnifies problems to the point where it's not just *any* lion. It's not just a thirsty or starving lion wandering into the suburbs. No, this is a *killer* lion that stalks the streets, the places where people go, where groups meet, and where public activity takes place. Where life *happens*. But not for the sluggard, who in the next verse just turns over in his bed.

Do you see the self-fulfilling prophecy represented in these verses? The sluggard is too wise to read anything that he doesn't already think is true. He's too lazy to go out to places where life goes on. Easier to just stay inside, isolated—where dreams, not reality, rule.

Our prayer for you is that you'll realize wisdom doesn't come from pride, anxious fears, isolation, or dreaming. It's time to have the courage of faith. To get out and seek a community who will line the marathon of your life story.

Yes, making friends can be scary. It sure takes work to build relationships. And you must be prepared for some disappointment—not every person you meet is going to become a lifelong friend.

However, this is not the time to "get back in bed" and pretend that the challenges of marriage don't exist. This is the time to engage with others, to find new ways to connect so you don't go at this fight alone.

2. Serving Is a Great Space for Building Friendships

I remember a friend I had in high school. She wasn't the most popular girl in school, but she was one of the only people whom each person in our small graduating class not only liked but also considered a friend. When I talked with her about it, she said something I took to heart.

"I do what my mother said," she told me. "Get to the party early and volunteer to serve at the food table. That's the best way and place to meet people. Serve them. Ask them questions. Amazingly, that's what opens doors to relationships." (This was surprisingly similar to the advice my dad gave me when I went to my first, second, and millionth school dance. "Stand by the food," he said, "because boys like food.")

But how true those words from my friend are! Serving others, and serving with others, is a great way to build friendships. And as a married couple, you're looking for friends—not a date or someone to ask you to dance.

Friendship often happens when you're standing side by side with someone, sharing the same interest or focused on the same task. Because there aren't many "go off and do this alone" service opportunities, serving usually puts you near others.

If you have children, a great way to meet a pool of potential friends is by serving alongside other parents. That may be at your child's school when they need volunteers to help with events. Or at your church. Or in your neighborhood. Look at the places you go every day. What things can you do to serve others in those locations?

And don't forget that there are beautiful acts of service and hospitality that come when you open your home to others. One thing that helps Joey and me build relationships is something called "Dinner for Eight." We started off calling it "Kidless Couples" because it was hard to find other friends in their thirties who were married without kids, but as quickly as we could find couples, the kidless situation would change. And, praise God, this changed for us eventually as well.

Whatever you want to call it, invite three other couples over for dinner. Joey and I set this up as a once-a-month thing. The first month is at our house, and then dinner rotates to one of the other couples' homes the following month, and so on, until we've been around the circle.

Don't underestimate the power of friendship. C. S. Lewis, in his wonderful book *The Four Loves*, talks much about friendship:

> Friendship is the least jealous of loves. Two friends delight to be joined by a third, and three by a fourth, if only the newcomer is qualified to become a real friend. . . . In this, Friendship exhibits a glorious "nearness by resemblance" to Heaven itself where the very multitude of the blessed . . . increases the fruition which each has of God.[5]

3. Work toward Friendships with Those Who Reflect Joy

I encourage you and your spouse to always keep your eyes open for potential friends whose lives have that movement toward joy that we talked about in chapter 5. Remember that our progress through the Merge happens at the speed of joy. But I've also found that being friends with people who reflect joy really moves *friendships* along too. You probably know who I'm talking about—people who truly radiate joy, as opposed to those who keep their heads down and often seem to focus on their misery and depression. (Yes, I understand that these people need friends too, but it's still important to value joy and connection in our friendships. That should be your main focus, even as we understand that we should reflect love and kindness to everyone.)

Remember Psalm 16:11, which reminds us that in God's presence "is fullness of joy." We should strive to be in relationships with those who seek to be close to God's presence.

I understand that this isn't always easy. Sometimes it's difficult to build friendships, and especially the kind of friendships that reflect joy into your life. But this is important. Be resilient, standing back up after challenging circumstances push you down—such as when trying to build a friendship fails. That happens. But remember that the needs around you—the needs you can help meet by serving and reflecting joy to others—will always be there. Keep moving forward.

Know how to recognize when a friendship probably isn't going to happen. If a couple has made an excuse not to meet for the fourth time, then give them some space. Know that in the same way you and your spouse may step back from others, another couple who is desiring (but afraid of) friendship might be stepping back as well.

Be resilient in looking for ways to serve and in looking for people who reflect joy. And remember that Merge Mates are hugely important in every stage of life.

Along the Road

I still have the picture of my father and me holding up our half-marathon medals. I still remember all the "help" I got from those awful rock bands playing along the course. (Hey, at least they were enthusiastic!) Most of all, I still remember that I didn't have to cross that finish line alone.

You don't have to run this race alone either. Put the five Merge Tools together, and watch your relationship with your spouse grow. See the Merge Moments that once seemed daunting and unending fade into the long-term love and attachment you long for.

Before we move on to plotting the course of the Merge, let's look at what you've done so far:

- You've given your Merge (and the Mergenado it creates) a name, *identifying a specific challenge* that you're facing together (chapter 3).
- You've realized how small acts of *attachment* can shrink huge emotional mountains (chapter 4).
- You've begun to understand that the Merge moves at the *speed of joy* (chapter 5).
- You're appreciating, once again, the *strengths God has given your spouse* as things that complete you, not defeat you (chapter 6).

- You've learned the importance of *untying knots and striving to repair your relationship* (chapter 7).
- And you've explored the significance of serving and doing life together with friends, family, and other *Merge Mates* during every stage of your life (chapter 8).

In the next chapter, we'll personalize your Merge Tools and put them all together into your very own Merge Map.

Revisiting Ben and Jenna

When we left Ben and Jenna (earlier in this chapter), it was clear that they needed to find some Merge Mates to end the isolation that their move and the COVID-19 pandemic had caused. So they decided to make some big decisions.

"We decided to give ourselves six months," Jenna shared. "In those six months, we would do everything we could think of to make friends and break out of our isolated bubble."

"We'd invite anyone we met over for dinner or to go for a walk," Ben added. "As things began to open up, we'd invite people to get a cup of coffee, join us at church, or meet up at a restaurant."

Ben also decided to spend some of his extra time—when he wasn't looking for a job—volunteering at a food bank. The local food bank had a great need. And he had extra time.

Ben and Jenna were intentional. And six months later, they discovered they weren't alone anymore. They'd begun to connect with others and build community right where God had moved them. But He soon provided an even better job opportunity for both Ben and Jenna back home in California—just miles away from their friends and family.

"Even though we ended up back home, what we learned in that season was critical," Jenna explained. "We know now that no matter what comes, we cannot, and should not, try to do it alone. We need people to walk with us. To keep us accountable. To encourage us. Even just to have fun with us!"

Ben and Jenna are now taking their job to build Merge Mates seriously and are always on the lookout for other couples who may be searching for ways to connect as well.

Your Date Night

Don't wait! Find one other couple and plan a time to meet with them. You can go to dinner or cook something at home. Or keep it simple and just do dessert and coffee after the kids are in bed. If you sense a connection and a real friendship brewing, ask them if they'd be willing to help you navigate the Merge together. Consider reading through *The Merge for Marriage* together.

Bring another couple into your journey. It's time to stop going it alone. Before you shoot the idea down, remember that so many are looking for connection. Especially today. So ask! The worst thing someone can say is no, but we think you'll be surprised at how excited and ready other couples are to connect.

As you consider which other couples to connect with, discuss the following questions with your spouse:

1. Who are the Merge Mates we can rely on in our marriage?
2. Do we need to be more intentional about building community in this season? What might that look like?
3. What couple should we ask to help us make the Merge?
4. How do we feel about starting a small group of Merge Mates and walking through the challenges of the Merge with others?

9

Making Your Merge Map

WE'VE TALKED ABOUT FIVE TOOLS that can help you make the Merge. While I hope that the date nights at the end of each chapter are already helping you put the five tools into practice, it's time to introduce you to the Merge Map as well.

The Merge Map is designed to give you a clear plan for moving from information to transformation, helping you not only to name your Merge and deal with the Mergenado cycle it creates but also to move this material out of the book and into your home.

How does the Merge Map work? Using the five tools we've talked about in part 2 of this book, you'll fill out your own custom Merge Map. (See this book's appendix, which begins on page 153.) Our goal is for you to clearly see how the five Merge Tools work together to help you take on the Merge.

You *can* skip right to the map to get started. However, the information in this chapter will help you fill out your Merge Map correctly.

Let's get started.

Your Merge Map

At the top of your Merge Map, you will see a place where you can write the name you've given your Merge. You'll also see three key dates: a thirty-day check-in, a sixty-day check-in, and a ninety-day check-in.

Later, I'll explain how the check-ins will work. But for now, look at the calendar and pick three dates (thirty, sixty, and ninety days from now), and block out a few hours on each day to talk about the Merge. It's okay if they aren't exactly thirty, sixty, or ninety days from now, but try to stick to that time frame as closely as possible.

Let's start with the first box, "Defining Our Mergenado."

Defining Your Mergenado

In the first box of the Merge Map, you and your spouse will write what happens when you first find yourselves being sucked into your Mergenado.

You should have already discussed this during your date night (see page 46), but if you haven't yet, this is the time. Even if you've talked about it before, take some time to review. Then write it right there in your Merge Map.

Most of us have one major pattern, or Mergenado, that is the dominant storm in our marriage. However, if you notice any additional Mergenadoes twisting around in your relationship, make sure you capture them in your Merge Map too.

The good news is that when we do this, we often realize that we don't have a hundred problems—we really only have one or two big ones. This makes our objectives in taking on the Merge clearer, and it helps them feel much more attainable, too.

Remember: It's often not about the towels, the dishwasher, the budget, or any number of smaller problems that come up. Rather, think more deeply. *Consider the need behind the deed.* In other words, there's an issue. And there are also triggering circumstances that often launch the Mergenado into action.

Take your time. Using the prompts below, name and describe your Mergenado from start to finish:

- Name your Mergenado.
- What starts the Mergenado?
- Describe what happens as your Mergenado spins. How do you respond? How does your spouse respond?
- What's the emotional need behind your Mergenado?
- How does your Mergenado stop?
- What damage does your Mergenado cause? How do you each end up feeling?

Stopping the Storm

In the same column, you'll see a smaller box called "Stopping the Storm." This is where you will write two things:

1. Your warning signal. Remember the Mergenado alarm, name, or phrase you can use when you see the storm beginning to form? That's your warning signal.
2. One small practical step you will each take to stop the Mergenado from spinning.

If you need a refresher about anything in this column, go back and revisit your first Merge Tool, which is found in chapter 3.

Now let's look at the second column, "Shrinking the Mountains."

Shrinking the Mountains

In this column, write several ways that you can build attachment into your marriage, things that will help your spouse know that your hand is on their shoulder.

If you can only come up with one idea, that's a great start. But we encourage people to work hard and come up with ten small, specific things you can do to help your spouse feel like you are there. From calling and checking in when you're at work to going for a walk together after dinner. To giving a five-minute back rub (with no strings attached). To praying for and with your spouse.

After you have your list, do a few of the actions every week for the next ninety days. You don't have to go in order or even announce to your spouse which one you are going to do. Just start mixing these positive things into your daily life. And there's room for more! Keep adding to the list as you think of new ways to help shrink the mountains in your marriage.

If you need a refresher about anything in this column, look again at the second Merge Tool in chapter 4.

Adding Joy

Now brainstorm ten ways that you can begin adding joy into your marriage, and put them in the third column. Start implementing these ideas, perhaps focusing on one per week for the next ninety days. If you get stuck or need more help filling out this column, revisit the third Merge Tool in chapter 5.

Okay, we are almost done—so hang with me! Let's move over to the fourth column, "Valuing Your Spouse's Strengths."

Valuing Your Spouse's Strengths

In this column, take some time to list five strengths you see in your spouse. Once you've written them down, grab your spouse's hand and read these strengths out loud.

Make sure that you stick to five. You can always add more later. But five is a good number for this. (And there's nothing worse than feeling like you couldn't come up with as many as your spouse.) This isn't about quantity; it's about quality.

If you need help filling out this column, reference the fourth Merge Tool in chapter 6.

Now let's look at the top box of that fifth column, the one titled "Untying Knots and Repairing."

Untying Knots and Repairing

In this column, come together to identify any knots that need to be untied or hurts that need to be repaired in your marriage.

Helpful hint: If your spouse says it, you need to address it. Don't assume that because it doesn't bother you, it's not an issue. If both of you aren't happy—ain't nobody happy.

Schedule a time to walk through the repair steps in chapter 7. Or, if these are bigger issues, make a call to a friend, pastor, or counselor to begin this process.

Next, at the bottom of the fifth column, move to the section titled "Our Merge Mates."

Recognizing Merge Mates

In this box, each of you will write down one person outside your marriage whom you can ask to help keep you accountable as you go through the Merge. Wives should choose a woman, and husbands should choose a man.

Remember, we are not designed to do life alone. And it's incredibly hard on your spouse to be the only person who is keeping you accountable. So pick up the phone and ask someone you trust to check in with you once a week for the next three months as you work through your Merge Map.

Helpful hint: Remember that this is not the time to pick the friend who is great at having fun but not so great at asking you the hard questions. Or the friend who struggles to make good on commitments. If you really want to grow, it will serve you well to seek out the friend who is truly going to help you follow through.

Bonus points: Ask your spouse which of your friends would be a good choice. You still need to agree with your spouse about whom to choose, of course, because ultimately you are the one who will be interacting with this friend. But your spouse may help you see things you don't.

Once you've identified your Merge Mate, have him or her ask you these three questions every week:

1. How did you do this week?
2. What can you do to make next week better?
3. Is there anything you need help with to get where you want to be?

Then give the friend permission to ask your spouse one question: How did your spouse do this week?

I get it. That's scary. It's personal. It's vulnerable. And it's probably awkward. But if you want to change, get someone else involved.

If you need any help finding Merge Mates or want a refresher on what this can look like, revisit chapter 8.

Before we move on to the next section, there is one more box beside "Our Merge Mates" that you need to fill out: "When We Get Stuck."

When We Get Stuck

In the next chapter, we are going to go into detail about this topic. So you can wait to fill out this part of the map until you've read chapter 10.

But, as a quick summary, this box is where you and your spouse will list three things you can do if (or more likely *when*) you get stuck along the way.

You may not get stuck as often as Joey and I do. However, the time will likely come when you do. These moments can be incredibly frustrating and quite emotional. After all, you've both been working so hard. If all that effort didn't work, what will?

That's why you need to plan for that moment now before you reach that emotional place. It's always easier to see a way out before you get stuck. It's much harder to discover one when the pressure is on.

So take some time with your spouse and write down three things you can do to get some extra help if you find yourself in a place where things aren't going as planned. For example, Joey and I listed these things:

1. Meet with a counselor for six sessions.
2. Ask Grandma to watch Lincoln for a weekend while we have a staycation to reconnect.
3. Meet for a meal with our Merge Mates, the Buskirks. And let them share what they see in our marriage.

Next, list three things you can *each* do if you get stuck individually.

At times I've needed extra help. And at times Joey's needed extra help. And at times we've needed to get help together. I can tell you that planning *what* we will do, both individually and as a couple, when things inevitably get hard has helped us more times than we can count.

So know how and when to step away from the emotions of the moment, and have an agreed-upon plan to get some extra assistance when you're really stuck. Again, if you need more help with this, read chapter 10 before you fill out this section of your Merge Map.

Finally, let's look at the last box, the box at the bottom called "Committed to Doing Something Great."

There Is Still a Great "What's Next?"

I realize that unless it's a whodunit mystery, most of us tend to skip the last chapter of a book. After all, in most cases it's just a recap of everything we've already learned. Not a place where new information is found.

Well, not in this book. To fill out this last section of your Merge Map, you'll need to read through chapter 11. There you'll discover not only the importance of putting what you've learned into practice but also how you can help another couple struggling through the Merge.

So leave this one blank for now, and after you read chapter 11, "The Call to Do Something Great," come back and finish your Merge Map.

Okay, those are the basics on filling out your Merge Map. Now let's circle back to those check-in dates you penciled in at the top.

Check-In Time

You've already picked three dates that are thirty, sixty, and ninety days from now. And I hope you have placed those dates on your calendar. When those dates roll around, here's what you are going to do: Plan to spend two hours (max) somewhere public, like the food court, a coffee shop, or a restaurant. Once you get there, pull out your Merge Map. Grab your spouse's hand. Yes, for real, try to hold your spouse's hand while talking—as if you're actually, physically supporting him or her at the bottom of a steep hill.

Take turns asking each other the following questions:

1. How am I doing with my part in the Mergenado?
2. How am I doing at building attachment in our relationship?
3. How am I doing at adding joy to our marriage?
4. How am I doing at making you feel valued and appreciated?
5. Is my Merge Mate working out?
6. Have we sought to repair our relationship when our attachment seems damaged?
7. Do we need to do anything to help us move forward? (See the box "When We Get Stuck.")

And if you have time, ask this final question:

8. What is one small thing I can do this week that would bless you?

Make sure you both get a chance to share and to listen.

Golden Retrievers and Beavers, look over the questions a few days before each check-in and take the time to think through your answers. The check-in isn't the moment to ask for more time to think but to show up ready and prepared to share.

Lions and Otters, verbally process your answers a few days before the check-in so you'll be clear when you share. Focus on considering the impact of your words before you speak them.

While I hope and pray that these check-ins are full of only positive experiences, the reality is that they aren't always that way. In fact, at times Joey and I both have had to say something that wasn't easy for the other person to hear. If that happens to you, be glad you're in a public place. (It's harder to yell there because it's incredibly embarrassing, and they may even kick you out.) Remember, this is a check-in—a time to talk and adjust your course, not throw in the towel.

If you have a not-so-great check-in? Look at the "When We Get Stuck" box, and get to work. Don't be afraid to ask for help. You are not in this alone.

Why Ninety Days?

You may be asking why we want you to focus on your Merge Map for ninety days. Remember, this is about transformation. It takes a long time to form new habits. Throw in some weekends and holidays, a visiting mother-in-law, challenges with parenting, or the dog getting sick, and you'll start to realize why you've planned for a grace-based ninety days.

Of course, we pray that you will see results long before that. But ninety days can give you and your spouse the time to feel confident with your new responses. To see growth. To begin taking incredible strides toward successfully making the Merge.

Now that you know how to fill out and use your Merge Map, let's move on to that critical chapter—the one that will help you know what to do when you get stuck.

Your Date Night

If you haven't yet finished filling out what you can of your Merge Map, take some time to do that now. (Come back after reading the next two chapters so that you can finish the last two sections.)

Here's a fun idea: Set up a blanket/pillow/sofa-cushion fort in your bedroom or living room as you complete your Merge Map to enhance that feeling of coming together and forming a "battle plan" to take on the Merge.

Wisdom to Stay on the Map

THE GOAL OF THIS BOOK isn't just information but also transformation. We've said that several times already. But repetition is often the key to learning.

You've done a great job moving toward transformation just by getting this far in the book! You've worked through the five Merge Tools, and you've hopefully had some fun and helpful Merge-themed date nights. You've begun to fill out your Merge Map, which will pull together key things you've learned into a single visual display—a tool you can refer to, pray over, and follow as you make the Merge.

But there's a problem. Eventually something will knock you off course. You must not stop running toward the end zone when you're at the one-yard line or fumble the ball before you score. So this chapter is here to help.

Yes, navigating the Merge can be messy. It doesn't happen overnight. And if we find ourselves falling back into old patterns after taking steps to improve our relationship, we may believe that nothing has changed after all. But real change *has* happened, even if we feel defeated by our slipups and mistakes.

It's like doing well on a diet or eating plan. You're doing really well for a long time, and then you fall back into some bad habits for Thanksgiving or your birthday or, in my case, Taco Tuesday. And how easy it is, with tacos everywhere, to feel like you just blew everything!

Do not believe the lies. Recognize that your progress is real. You haven't fallen back into your old self. You've just had a bad taco day. (Or a *good* taco day, I suppose, depending on the tacos in question, but you get my point.)

You are just facing a bad case of normal—like when a Mergenado shows up after months of clear, sunny days.

Let me give you another example. Picture someone who views his identity and worth as maybe a two out of ten. He believes he's at, or near, the bottom. Now give that person a promotion. Overnight, put him in a job that rewards him and expects him to have the confidence, identity, and strength of an eight or a nine. (But remember, he's convinced he's just a two!) Very often, this will create a sort of honeymoon effect, meaning that the person will live up to his new role for a short time. But soon, you'll see him crater or dramatically fall back to where he (likely falsely) believes he really is.

It's like going down a black diamond ski slope for the first time. The skier may do well for the first third of the run. Everything feels great. But as she looks around, her eyes seem to open. *This is really steep! And fast! Maybe I'm not that good a skier. Maybe I should never have let my friends talk me into taking this black diamond run to begin with!* And that's just about when she crashes.

This does not have to be you. In large part because you've already built a great foundation by working through the tools in this book. A foundation not just for knowledge but for active application of these tools.

Each relationship-building tool you've learned and practiced can help you get safely down the slope, or in this case, through the Merge. But it is a common, human, predictable experience for us to feel like we're in over our heads or to question whether the growth and change we are making is real and going to last.

So what can you do?

At StrongFamilies, we train our life coaches to help people practice something called *learned hopefulness*. Learned hopefulness is the opposite of a clinical designation called learned helplessness, in which people are actually conditioned to be helpless. Think of children raised under an overbearing parent, one who does everything for their children and rarely allows them to learn how to do things themselves.

Learned helplessness is what we see, for example, with the people of Israel. For hundreds of years, they'd been in bondage and captivity in Egypt. Then: freedom! At first, they did great. God was obviously moving miraculously on their behalf. From bringing the plagues that made Pharaoh release the Israelites to pulling back the Red Sea, saving them from Pharaoh's army, God was clearly doing some incredible things.

With so much going for them—not to mention the King of the Universe leading the way—everything should be great, right? They were free. Headed for the Promised Land. Filled with the certainty of God's Spirit going in front of them by day and by night. They even had daily meals through the manna God provided.

But remember that they had endured years of feeling and being helpless. And then they began hitting rough patches. Like not having enough water. Or growing tired of all that manna. And instead of moving forward, the people began to grumble.

"We need to go back to Egypt! It wasn't so bad there!"

Which was a total lie. But much like that person who believes he's a two, the Israelites felt hopeless. And a little bit panicky.

When that happened, they did the only thing they knew how to do. They returned to helplessness. Though they knew God had done some miraculous things, they fell back into questioning their identity, as well as God's concern for them. The Israelites lost their trust in God's character and His provision for them, so much so that they built a false god in the form of a golden calf.

You'd think they would have learned their lesson after forty years of being led by God through the wilderness. But then, when God said, "Go and take the Promised Land," ten of the twelve spies sent to scope out the situation came back proclaiming messages of helplessness: "The people there are too big! There are too many of them! God can't possibly mean what He said. We can't take this land. There's no way." They fell right back toward helplessness—heads down, not up.

If that is learned helplessness, then what is learned hopefulness? And how can we move toward that instead?

Learned hopefulness is an attitude based on the reality of God's Word and His love. This attitude gives us not just the joy we talked about in chapter 5 but also the confidence of knowing we're not facing things alone. We may fall down, but He can help us get back up. This attitude helps build in us a spirit of resilience—one that says, even in the midst of challenges, *We can do this!*

First, consider the impact of this kind of learned hopefulness. Do you know anyone who named their son Shammua? Or Shaphat? Or Igal? Those were three of the ten spies who came back from looking over the Promised Land and said, "Forget it. We can't do this."

On the other hand, do you know anyone who named their son Joshua or Caleb? They were the two who said, "Bring it on." Caleb even said something like "I'll go take the high country, the toughest place to win" (see Joshua 14:12). That's the very definition of hopefulness.

No, you don't have to change your name or your kids' names to Joshua or Caleb. But you do need to model the kind of faith and courage that they showed. To believe in the reality they saw, based on God's Word. There would be challenges. There would be tough days. But they had a great, unchanging, loving, never-leave-you-ever God. He would be with them through this fight!

When the ten pessimistic spies came back, they magnified the problems ahead of them. They saw the forces in front of them and said, in effect, "We've seen them, and they're like giants! We're nothing but grasshoppers compared to them!" (see Numbers 13:25-33).

Now, Joshua and Caleb didn't minimize the challenge. But they held on to the One who was supporting them. They fully believed in His wisdom and plan. They were confident that the Lord had their front and their back. That He would fulfill His promises, including the promise of the beautiful land in front of them.

Consider these words from the apostle Paul: "I am sure of this, that he who began a good work in you will bring it to completion at the day of Jesus Christ" (Philippians 1:6). Paul wasn't hesitant about voicing his opinions. Even so, this to Paul was a rock-solid fact: God isn't done doing the mighty work He has promised to do.

Reflect on that truth. God isn't done with us. Even if we've been stuck in the Merge a long time. Or only gotten through part of it. Or just had a bad day that makes us feel like we've slid back to the beginning of the Chutes and Ladders game. Hold on to the light of the truth—the truth that God is still at work in your lives: "Little children, you are from God and have overcome them, for he who is in you is greater than he who is in the world" (1 John 4:4).

God gives you the insight and power to make the Merge:

- to recognize and stop your Mergenado;
- to know His hand is on your shoulder as you keep your hand on your spouse's shoulder;
- to bring you joy for the journey that can transform your thinking and your lives;
- to help you view each other's strengths as valuable contributions to your marriage team;
- to help you repair your relationship and release you both from all the knots that weaken your bond; and
- to equip you to build a community of Merge Mates in which each member cheers the others on toward unity, oneness, and love.

We believe that you will face challenges and challenging days. The Merge Map you made isn't magic. But we also believe that you *can* and you *will* be like the two spies who chose hopefulness by trusting the God of hope.

With that in mind, we'd like to share with you some wisdom for your journey, a little encouragement to replace any fear of falling back to feeling like you're only a two out of ten.

Staying on Your Merge Map

First, beware of resting too long. Now, there is nothing wrong with rest. Rest is good. After all, the Lord rested on the seventh day of creation, modeling for us an important priority in our lives. And Jesus observed the day of rest too—not taking a pause from doing good, but nevertheless resting and encouraging His disciples to rest.

Yet there's something important about rest that often gets ignored. We forget that rest comes *after* work. Rest is the reward. And making the Merge, as we've said from the first chapter, is going to take work. The work comes before the rest.

It's not wrong to sit down or kick back or even binge-watch an entire season of your favorite show. But that's for *after* doing what you need to do. Rest is intended to be refreshing, powerful, and temporary. Resting for too long becomes a passive way of giving up. Here's a picture of what I mean:

I passed by the field of a sluggard,
   by the vineyard of a man lacking sense,
and behold, it was all overgrown with thorns;
   the ground was covered with nettles,
   and its stone wall was broken down.
Then I saw and considered it;
   I looked and received instruction.
A little sleep, a little slumber,
   a little folding of the hands to rest,

and poverty will come upon you like a robber,
   and want like an armed man.

PROVERBS 24:30-34

Look at those last four lines. If the sluggard rests too long, it makes it easy for poverty to sneak up on him like a robber, and then escaping his impoverished condition will be like fighting an enemy holding a shield and a sword. It will be very difficult to get through those defenses to take back the prosperous field he once had.

Don't fall into that position. You've got your plan to make the Merge. You've got a vision and a hope—that you can indeed be two-who-become-one. You can move forward into that promised place of growth and spiritual and relational strength. But beware of taking too many breaks from doing good things, from making those small, slight changes that can have a big impact. You may wake up someday and find that things are falling apart.

True rest isn't about laziness or giving up. True rest renews us for the job ahead: building a strong home and protecting it. It's the kind of rest that doesn't let the weeds move in or the walls fall down. Giving up just leads us to where we are no longer secure, where we face urgent needs that are stubborn and unyielding. That's not real rest.

A second important thing to consider as you follow your Merge Map is how fun it can be to go "off-roading."

One of my favorite places to go off-roading is in beautiful Sedona, Arizona. (How beautiful? Well, five routes on the US government's "National Scenic Byways and All-American Roads" list are in Arizona.[1] One of these drives takes you around the north rim of the Grand Canyon. Another takes you up and around the amazing red rock formations of Sedona.)

Most people see Sedona via the normal, paved, and very crowded drive around the red rock formations. Yes, they are breathtaking, even from the highway. But it's more fun to get right in among those rocks, which means taking dirt roads that in many places would shatter a typical car's suspension or bash up the gas tank. Hence all the off-road vehicle rentals available in the area.

Having the right vehicle is essential. It's incredibly fun to go up a high hill or down a rocky and challenging path. But even before you drive up or down those heart-pounding slopes, there's something very important you need to do. You need to slow down—or even stop, depending on the vehicle—and put the transmission in low gear or four-wheel drive. Then you need to continue to adjust your speed to match the challenge of the trail.

The more difficult the terrain, the slower you have to go. While slowing down may sound tedious, it is the very thing that allows you to navigate some of the hardest stretches of road. And your reward is reaching some of the most beautiful views imaginable.

If you go too fast, even with the right vehicle, you can end up stuck in the mud or stranded with a damaged car. This prevents you not just from seeing the views but from moving forward at all.

Slowing down as you navigate tough challenges can be so useful in making the Merge. It's easy to make snap judgments. Yet in Proverbs we're told, "If one gives an answer before he hears, it is his folly and shame" (Proverbs 18:13).

I know we've said that joy will help speed up the Merge. But here we're talking about those hairpin turns and white-knuckle drops. These require a decrease in speed. More listening. Reflecting. Asking questions. And working on taking a breath before blowing off steam.

Sometimes You'll Need a Full Pit Stop

As Joey and I stepped into the new realm of parenting, we continually found ourselves laughing about things we were doing that we had never done before.

One of these new things was something we began to call a "full pit stop." This was when our son needed an outfit change, a diaper change, and a bottle—all at the same time.

When one of us called out "Full pit stop!" we burst into action.

One of us grabbed a diaper, the other an outfit. One of us heated up the milk, while the other finalized the clothing swap. Although Lincoln was never very happy during a full pit stop, our little man was back to his happy, giggly self as soon as Joey and I had him dry, clean, and full. In fact, we started timing ourselves and are proud to say that at our peak, we could get Lincoln dry, clean, and eating in less than sixty seconds. (Yes, you sometimes have to do these little competitive things to make the repetitive parts of parenting more fun.)

While we turned it into a game, the reality is that if we didn't address these problems, things could go from bad to worse just as quickly as we could solve them. If you've ever had an inconsolable five-month-old, you know what I mean.

The same is true for our marriages. The Merge adds wear and tear to our relationships. And sometimes the check-engine, fuel, or tire-pressure light turns on. If we stop and deal with the problem, it's often small, simple, and easy to fix.

If we ignore the problem, it grows. And soon we aren't looking at an oil change but an engine replacement. Or we run out of gas—miles away from the nearest gas station. Or we discover that there was a nail in our tire that made it go flat as we were driving on the freeway.

I want to encourage you to pay attention to the warning lights that may come on in your relationship. It's not a sign of weakness or failure to take your car to a mechanic. Just like it's not a sign of weakness or failure to decide it's time to meet with a counselor, phone a friend, or ask for some extra help.

Kids Are God's Little Spies

Finally, I know that some of you reading this may not have kids yet. Or maybe you're like Joey and me, and you are still new to this journey of parenting. But kids or not, don't skip this section. There is still a big, important truth here that will help you make the Merge.

If there are kids in your home, know that while you make the Merge, your kids are watching you like God's little spies. Actually, many people will be looking at you when you make your Merge. We've already talked about that cloud of witnesses (mentioned in Hebrews 12:1) who surround us and are cheering us on. But there are other groups watching you try to make the Merge as well—like your family and extended family, who can and will see a difference in how you treat each other. There are also close friends and Merge Mates, who cheer you on and see how you value each other's strengths in ways you didn't before. You may even find that as you make the Merge, those at work notice that you're not so distracted with all the emotional challenges at home. That you're more focused. More productive. Even more joyful.

And, of course, God's little spies are watching you all the time. You can say anything you want, have any number of Bible verses hanging on the walls of your home. But your kids know if you're faking it. They know whether you're really making the Merge. Here's an example.

On one of your date nights, watch the movie *Oliver Twist*. While there are several versions of this story, some with lots of music, make sure you get the 1948 black-and-white version directed by David Lean. Yes, I want you to watch a black-and-white movie. (If you have kids, you'll have to explain to them the marvel of color television and then maybe answer a million questions about how you ever survived in a world without the ability to stream movies on your phone.)

Oliver Twist is a wonderful story of a group of downtrodden street orphans in England during the early days of the industrial revolution. These kids are being taken advantage of big-time, laboring in a miserable workhouse under a terrible headmaster whom all of them fear. And then one boy, Oliver, dares to say, "Please, sir, I want some more."

That's "more" of their one bowl per day of gruel. They're all hungry. But never has anyone asked for *more*. Until Oliver does—an act of defiance that sets the rest of the story's events in motion.

But watch closely to see what else is here in the gloomy parish workhouse. You'll see the headmaster and his cronies. Their dinner table is filled with meat, cheese, and bread. They're regularly having a feast, while the boys they're supposed to be shepherding are given nothing but bowls of gruel. It's supposed to be a Christian institution, and you may notice words painted on the brick walls: *God is good. God is just. God is life.*

The 1968 musical version of this story, *Oliver!*, shows the boys in a great stone hall filled with long tables. As the camera zooms out, you'll see words written on the wall in huge block letters: GOD IS LOVE.

These words may be written on the wall, but from everything else we see on screen, it seems clear that this workhouse is anything but Christian. Not because the propositional statement written on the wall isn't true. God—the real God of Scripture—*is* love. But the boys in that workhouse aren't experiencing any part of the reality of those words. Their experiential truth is duplicity—the headmaster acting charitable when the authorities are around but horrible when it's just him and the boys.

That's why we're so proud and encouraged by your working through this book, your commitment to making your Merge. And doing so in a way that lets your kids, and those around you, see it in your words and your actions. Because kids (and discerning friends) can see right through people who are just image managers—people who have a public self and a private self that are often worlds apart.

If you've got kids, they need parents who are committed to loving like Jesus and moving forward with propositional truth. Left-brain theology and practice and right-brain joy and attachment. That combination makes love *real* to a kid because that love is displayed authentically in your life.

Ask yourselves, "Are we being loving, calm, and non-anxious parents to our children?"

This happens as you reflect love, acceptance, and joy—as you merge and grow closer to each other.

It's our job to model security for our kids—giving them the

confidence to meet the challenges that will come in their lives without being afraid that everything will fall apart if things aren't perfect.

Okay, that was our last word of wisdom for staying on track to make the Merge. But we're not quite finished. There is one more chapter: one more crucial task that will not only strengthen your and your spouse's ability to make the Merge but also help other couples do the same.

PART FOUR

Beyond Ourselves

The Call to Do Something Great

IN HIS BOOK *Everyone Communicates, Few Connect,* John C. Maxwell tells a powerful story about President Abraham Lincoln.

During the dark days of the Civil War, President Lincoln often went to a church not far from the White House. On one occasion, as he and a friend walked back to the White House, Lincoln was asked what he thought about the sermon.

"Well," Lincoln pondered, "it was well conceived and powerfully delivered."

"So you thought the preacher gave a great sermon?"

"No," Lincoln replied, "I thought it utterly failed."

When the man looked at him in shock, Lincoln explained, "It utterly failed because he never called us to do something great."[1]

I am certainly no Abraham Lincoln. But as we end our look at making the Merge, I would be totally remiss if I didn't call you to do something *great.*

What You've Done Is Pretty Great

By working through this whole book, what you've done for your relationship is pretty great. You've named your Merge. You've figured out your Mergenado. You've set up an early-warning system to keep from getting sucked into that cycle over and over again.

You've learned how to build attachment and shrink mountains by keeping your hand on your loved one's shoulder, and you've discovered how to move through your Merge while adding more joy to your relationship. You've realized how important it is to become a student of your loved one's strengths. You've learned the importance of repairing the bond between you and your spouse, and you've begun building a team of Merge Mates.

As you integrate these tools into your life, great things will happen. You'll move from information to transformation by God's love and grace.

But we were not made to merely build *ourselves* up. And that's where we'd like to end this book—by giving you a call to do something great.

Others Who Need to Make the Merge

It's so easy to stop after the question "What's in it for me?" has been answered. But remember what God wants us to do with our gifts and strengths. They're not just to build ourselves up but to help others, too:

> For by the grace given to me I say to everyone among you not to think of himself more highly than he ought to think, but to think with sober judgment, each according to the measure of faith that God has assigned. For as in one body we have many members, and the members do not all have the same function, so we, though many, are one body in Christ, and individually members one of another. Having gifts that differ according to the grace given to us, let us use

them: if prophecy, in proportion to our faith; if service, in
our serving; the one who teaches, in his teaching; the one
who exhorts, in his exhortation; the one who contributes, in
generosity; the one who leads, with zeal; the one who does
acts of mercy, with cheerfulness.

ROMANS 12:3-8

When the disciples were arguing over who was the greatest, Jesus
spoke to them His famous words about how the first shall be last and
the last first: "Let the greatest among you become as the youngest,
and the leader as one who serves. For who is the greater, one who
reclines at table or one who serves? Is it not the one who reclines at
table? But I am among you as the one who serves" (Luke 22:26-27).

This means that when we call you to do something great, we're
not talking about you "being great." We're talking about reaching out
and helping, blessing, and encouraging others who need your love
and help. Like friends you know who are battling the Merge.

By this point in the book, you've come so far in understanding
the Merge that you'll be shocked how often you see it popping up in
the relationships of those around you. And some of those people are
really struggling like Joey and I were, or perhaps like you were when
you first picked up this book.

So we're calling you to do something great.

To help just *one* other couple.

You probably have that couple in mind right now. So start today.
Set up a time to meet. Pray before you meet. And then share with
them a little about the Merge. Don't try to force-feed them everything
you've learned. That's like showing people all two thousand pictures
you took on your Norwegian cruise. That's punishment, not help.

Just bring up the idea of the Merge and talk about one of the tools
that has really helped you. Maybe even show them your Merge Map.
And then invite them to meet with you, if it would be helpful, to
further discuss this. Maybe even go through this book, one chapter
at a time.

You could also start a small group to read through this book. Your challenge is to not make this about *you*, but for you—as the Lord has built up and encouraged you—to reach out to *others*. Learning about how to make the Merge may be the most valuable gift you can give another couple.

We're Not Going Anywhere

None of us know the future. So we're going to say that Joey and I will be here "forever," even though it's only the Lord who knows our days and hours. Still, as long as the Lord gives us breath and strength and a platform for ministry, we'll be looking for ways to encourage you, your small group, your church, and your friends.

If there's any way we can be of help to you as you make the Merge—or help another couple make the Merge—just visit KariTrentStageberg.com. And don't forget to sign up for the free Making the Merge Challenge if you haven't already. We'd love to connect with you.

May the Lord bless, keep, and guide you! May you have wisdom for your Merge so that it passes quickly. And may your marriage be filled with joy and hands on each other's shoulders, more connected than ever before.

APPENDIX

The Merge Map

The Merge Map

The Name We've Given Our Merge

Defining Our Mergenado
Name and describe your Mergenado from start to finish:

Shrinking the Mountains
List ten ways you can build attachment:

Adding Joy
List ten ways you can add joy:

Stopping the Storm
What is our warning signal? How do we stop our Mergenado?

Committed to Doing Something Great:

**30-Day
Check-in Date**

**60-Day
Check-in Date**

**90-Day
Check-in Date**

_____   _____   _____

Valuing Your Spouse's Strengths
List five strengths you see in your spouse:

Untying Knots and Repairing
Are there any knots we need to untie or key areas we need to repair?

Our Merge Mates
Who will keep us accountable?

When We Get Stuck
What are three things we can agree to do if we get stuck, both individually and as a couple?

Acknowledgments

There are so many people I'd like to thank. First and foremost, I'd like to thank three people who took a chance in allowing this book to happen: Larry Weeden, Steve Johnson, and Dr. Greg Smalley. Without each of you believing in this project, it wouldn't exist. I am honored and humbled to be here, and I hope this book makes you proud—or at least confirms that you weren't losing your minds as you moved forward with *The Merge for Marriage*.

To Robin Jones Gunn: Thank you for your friendship, your encouragement, and your wisdom. Every time I wanted to quit, words *you* shared popped into my mind. Your books changed my life, and now you are helping raise up a new generation of authors. I pray that this blessing is multiplied tenfold over you.

To Vance Fry: Thank you for your patience, grace, and ability to understand my heart through what was sometimes a jumble of words—and to make the end product reflect all that. Without your careful edits, this book would not be what it is.

To Kelly Kimbro: Thank you for your help, support, and friendship.

To Haley Jersey: Without you, none of these opportunities would be here. Thank you for seeing something others didn't, and for working hard to move it into reality.

And to the couples who spent hours meeting with me to talk about their own journeys: Thank you for your trust, your vulnerability, and your willingness to do something great by sharing the painful parts of your stories in order to encourage others. I pray you are blessed beyond measure.

Another huge *Thank you!* goes out to my dad, an incredible cheerleader and a wonderful editor. Thank you for helping me grow, for giving me a chance to minister alongside you, and for modeling everything you teach. I love you, Daddy, and I pray that as this book blesses others, you will be encouraged to see the legacy you have built.

Also, to Joey: God has given me the best husband in the world, but he has also given Lincoln and Sawyer the best possible father. Thank you for joyfully jumping into full-time dad duty as I worked hard to finish this book. And thank you for providing honest feedback, even when I didn't want to hear it. And most of all, thank you for choosing to do the Merge with me every single day. I love you, I love you, I love you.

Kari Trent Stageberg

Notes

CHAPTER ONE | THAT FIRST LIFE-ALTERING MERGE MOMENT
1. Michael Fulwiler, "Managing Conflict: Solvable vs. Perpetual Problems," The Gottman Institute, https://www.gottman.com/blog/managing-conflict -solvable-vs-perpetual-problems.

CHAPTER THREE | YOUR FIRST MERGE TOOL: STOPPING THE MERGENADO
1. Sue Johnson, *Hold Me Tight: Seven Conversations for a Lifetime of Love* (New York: Little, Brown and Company, 2008), loc. 48 of 359, Apple Books.

CHAPTER FOUR | YOUR SECOND MERGE TOOL: MAKING MOUNTAINS SHRINK
1. C. S. Lewis, *Mere Christianity* (London: Geoffrey Bles, 1952; repr., New York: HarperCollins, 2017), 119–20.
2. Lewis, *Mere Christianity*, 132.
3. Lewis, *Mere Christianity*, 131.
4. Simone Schnall, Kent D. Harber, Jeanine K. Stefanucci, and Dennis R. Proffitt, "Social Support and the Perception of Geographical Slant," *Journal of Experimental Social Psychology* 44, no. 5 (September 2008): 1246–55, https://doi.org/10.1016/j.jesp.2008.04.011.
5. "Jack Needs Jill to Get Up the Hill: Perceptions Affected by Friendship," *The University of Virginia Magazine*, Fall 2009, https://uvamagazine.org/articles /jack_needs_jill_to_get_up_the_hill.

6. Sue Johnson, *Hold Me Tight: Seven Conversations for a Lifetime of Love* (New York: Little, Brown and Company, 2008), loc. 67–68 of 359, Apple Books.

CHAPTER FIVE | YOUR THIRD MERGE TOOL: MERGING AT THE SPEED OF JOY

1. Tania Lombrozo, "The Truth about the Left Brain/Right Brain Relationship," *13.7: Cosmos and Culture*, National Public Radio, December 2, 2013, https://www.npr.org/sections/13.7/2013/12/02/248089436/the-truth -about-the-left-brain-right-brain-relationship.

CHAPTER SIX | YOUR FOURTH MERGE TOOL: SPOTLIGHTING YOUR SPOUSE'S STRENGTHS

1. This chapter offers just a brief overview of the four personality types, but if you'd like to go deeper into this subject, I recommend an incredible book called *The Two Sides of Love: The Secret to Valuing Differences* by Gary Smalley and my father, John Trent. Their book *The Treasure Tree* explains these principles to younger readers with an adorable, entertaining story. At StrongFamilies, we also offer an online course and a life-coaching certification program based on the Connect Assessment. Visit StrongFamilies.com for more information.

2. Sue Johnson, *Hold Me Tight: Seven Conversations for a Lifetime of Love* (New York: Little, Brown and Company, 2008), 38.

3. Associated Press, "U.S. 400-Meter Relay Teams Doomed by Flubbed Handoffs, Fail to Qualify," *ESPN*, August 21, 2008, https://www.espn.com/olympics /summer08/trackandfield/news/story?id=3545991.

CHAPTER SEVEN | YOUR FIFTH MERGE TOOL: LEARNING TO UNTIE THE KNOT AND REPAIR

1. Sue Johnson, *Hold Me Tight: Seven Conversations for a Lifetime of Love* (New York: Little, Brown and Company, 2008), loc. 53 of 359, Apple Books.

2. Michael W. Kraus, Cassey Huang, and Dacher Keltner, "Tactile Communication, Cooperation, and Performance: An Ethological Study of the NBA," *Emotion* 10, no. 5 (October 2010): 745–49, https://doi.org/10.1037/a0019382.

CHAPTER EIGHT | ADDING MERGE MATES TO YOUR JOURNEY

1. Howard Gleckman, "The High Cost of Loneliness: The Other Price Older Americans Are Paying for Covid-19," *Forbes*, March 25, 2021, https://www.forbes.com/sites/howardgleckman/2021/03/25/the-high -cost-of-loneliness-the-other-price-older-adults-are-paying-for-covid-19.

2. Marc Agronin, "What Covid-19 Taught Us about the High Cost of Isolation," *Wall Street Journal*, April 10, 2021, https://www.wsj.com/articles/covid-19 -isolation-11618005941.

3. Jacob Sweet, "The Loneliness Pandemic: The Psychology and Social Costs of Isolation in Everyday Life," *Harvard Magazine*, January–February 2021, https://www.harvardmagazine.com/2021/01/feature-the-loneliness-pandemic.
4. "Facts Are Stubborn Things," *Quote Investigator*, June 28, 2010, https://quoteinvestigator.com/2010/06/18/facts-stubborn.
5. C. S. Lewis, *The Four Loves* (London: Geoffrey Bles, 1960; repr., New York: Harcourt, Brace & Co., 1991), 61–62.

CHAPTER TEN | WISDOM TO STAY ON THE MAP

1. "National Scenic Byways & All-American Roads," US Department of Transportation, https://fhwaapps.fhwa.dot.gov/bywaysp/byways.

CHAPTER ELEVEN | THE CALL TO DO SOMETHING GREAT

1. Story retold based on John C. Maxwell, *Everyone Communicates, Few Connect: What the Most Effective People Do Differently* (Nashville: Thomas Nelson, 2010), chap. 9.